Jazz Phrasing

A Workshop for the Jazz Vocalist

Dr. Gloria Cooper and Don Sickler

SECOND FLOOR MUSIC

CD track listing

A Jazz Phrasing Workshop for the Vocalist

There are 85 tracks on the accompanying CD. Each track is listed below and referenced on the following contents page. The track numbers are also found on each page which describes the track or shows a corresponding music example. Many of the tracks start with a tuning note to give you your first pitch.

My Little Sherri

1. ♩= *ca.* 118 trumpet melody
2. trumpet & vocal syllables
3. rhythm section alone
4. ♩= *ca.* 122 trumpet melody
5. hear the lyric (Angela DeNiro sings)
6. rhythm section alone
7. ♩= *ca.* 140 trumpet melody
8. vocal syllables
9. rhythm section alone
10. ♩= *ca.* 160 trumpet melody
11. rhythm section alone
12. ♩= *ca.* 178 trumpet melody
13. hear the lyric
14. rhythm section alone
15. ♩= *ca.* 190 trumpet melody
16. rhythm section alone
17. ♩= *ca.* 190 trumpet melody (Charleston)
18. hear the lyric
19. rhythm section alone
20. ♩= *ca.* 160 lyric (rap) & beat box (Akil Dasan)

Beloved

21. Meredith d'Ambrosio sings
22. ♩= *ca.* 194 trumpet melody
23. rhythm section alone

You Know Who!

24. ♩= *ca.* 112 flugelhorn melody
25. rhythm section alone
26. Gloria Cooper sings the melody

Sweet And True

27. ♩= *ca.* 104 cymbal pattern
28. ensemble (first 4 bars)
29. piano playing figures with melody
30. piano not playing figures with melody
31. Gloria Cooper sings the melody

Do It Again

32. ♩= *ca.* 120 flugelhorn melody
33. vocal syllables
34. rhythm section alone
35. ♩= *ca.* 140 flugelhorn melody
36. hear the lyric
37. rhythm section alone
38. ♩= *ca.* 152 flugelhorn melody
39. hear the lyric
40. rhythm section alone
41. ♩= *ca.* 172 flugelhorn melody
42. flugelhorn & vocal syllables
43. duo: flugelhorn & vocal syllables
44. hear the lyric
45. rhythm section alone

Big Brown Eyes

46. ♩= *ca.* 138 flugelhorn melody
47. hear the lyric
48. rhythm section alone
49. ♩= *ca.* 168 flugelhorn melody
50. hear the lyric
51. rhythm section alone

I'm Movin' On

52. Judy Niemack sings the opening melody
53. fade in: out melody (Judy sings)
54. 2 against 3 (Judy sings)
55. rhythm section alone
56. walking bass, drums: brushes (Judy sings)
57. rhythm section alone
58. walking bass, drums: sticks (Judy sings)
59. rhythm section alone
60. jazz waltz (Judy sings)
61. rhythm section alone
62. medium Latin (trumpet melody)
63. medium Latin (Judy sings)
64. rhythm section alone
65. medium slow Latin (Judy sings)
66. rhythm section alone
67. smooth jazz (Judy sings)
68. rhythm section alone

Never Been In Love

69. example 1 (Gloria sings)
70. rhythm section alone
71. example 2 (Gloria sings)
72. rhythm section alone
73. example 3 (Gloria sings)
74. rhythm section alone
75. examples 4-9 (Gloria sings)
76. rhythm section alone

Your Day Is Comin'

77 - 80 trumpet plays complete arrangement

78. solo section
79. out melody
80. Coda
81. simplified background, tpt & rhythm section

82 - 85 complete arrangement, rhythm section

83. rhythm section alone, solos
84. rhythm section alone, out melody
85. rhythm section alone, Coda

A Workshop for the Jazz Vocalist

Jazz Phrasing

Dr. Gloria Cooper and Don Sickler

SECOND FLOOR MUSIC

Written by Dr. Gloria Cooper and Don Sickler

Book and cover design by Maureen Sickler
Music engraved by Osho Endo

The CD was recorded, mixed and mastered by Rudy Van Gelder
at Van Gelder Recording Studio, Inc. (except tracks 21, 26, 31)

Rhythm Section: Cecilia Coleman, piano; Tim Givens, bass;
Vince Cherico, drums; Jeanfrançois Prins, guitar
Trumpet & flugelhorn: Don Sickler
Vocalists: Gloria Cooper, Meredith d'Ambrosio, Akil Dasan,
Angela DeNiro, Judy Niemack

Track 21 is used by permission of Sunnyside Records
Tracks 26 and 31 are used by permission of GAC Music

130 West 28th Street, NY, NY 10001 www.secondfloormusic.com

Introduction

How do you define jazz phrasing? Webster's New Collegiate Dictionary defines *phrasing* as

a) Method of expression; phraseology; wording.
b) Music: Act, method, or result, of grouping the notes so as to form distinct musical phrases.

How you state the phrases of your musical message is very important. The feeling you put into your phrases is what will make your message memorable. Instrumental jazz artists have to create their phrases with melody and rhythm. Vocalists use those tools to shape yet another element, the lyric.

What we offer in this book is a practical, hands-on approach to fine-tuning important elements of *jazz phrasing*. This book/CD combination allows you to

- see how the music you hear is notated
- hear the melody played instrumentally, accompanied by an experienced jazz rhythm section
- hear many of the examples sung
- experiment on your own with rhythm section tracks

Our book defines two distinctive rhythmic styles of jazz phrasing. We call the two rhythmic styles *specific rhythm phrasing* and *open phrasing*.

Specific Rhythm Phrasing. This means that the rhythm of the melody must be adhered to in order to maintain the identity of the phrase. There are some examples where this is the case throughout a song, but most of the time songs will contain only sections or phrases that require specific rhythm phrasing.

Open Phrasing. This is the opposite situation. The rhythmic flow of the music can be freely interpreted by the vocalist. Open phrasing sections should be easily recognizable because the rhythmic notation of the melody is usually very general, using little or no syncopation.

Both of these two basic rhythmic styles can be present in a song. We will explore these two very different phrasing styles by looking at, listening to and analyzing specific examples drawn from music written by important instrumental jazz artists. All of the songs in this book started as instrumental compositions. With added lyrics, these songs are valuable additions to the vocal jazz repertoire.

The complete leadsheets for the song examples in this book are found in the ***Sing JAZZ!*** songbook (see page 53).

Specific Rhythm Phrasing
Interpreting Eighth Notes

Eighth notes are often found in sections that require specific rhythm phrasing. One of the first things to determine is how to approach the written eighth notes. Are they really even eighth notes as written, or should the eighth notes swing? If even eighths are called for, a tempo indication such as **Medium tempo (even eighth feel)** would certainly get the message across. But how do you interpret a tempo heading of **Medium swing**? How much should the eighth notes swing? Good question! You very likely have been told that eighth notes in jazz have to swing and should be played or sung with a triplet feeling. Following that school of thought, ♫ would be phrased this way: ♪♪♪ (3). However, if you convert all eighth notes to a literal triplet feel your phrases might sound corny and non-jazzy in many situations. The problem is, there is no consistent rule for singing or playing eighth notes. Every musical situation should be evaluated individually. The tempo and the style of accompaniment have a lot to do with how melodic eighth notes could be phrased. A solid background of listening to jazz is helpful in hearing and understanding the subtle nuances which determine how phrases are interpreted stylistically and rhythmically. The audio examples we've included here should help you make a connection between what you hear, what you see in music notation, and how to perform it.

Let's take a fresh look at melodic eighth notes in jazz. We'll start by examining different ways to phrase eighth notes in a medium tempo (swing) song, focusing on the differences between swing eighth notes and more even eighth notes. ***My Little Sherri***, taken from the songbook publication ***Sing JAZZ!***, was first written and recorded as an instrumental composition by the great jazz tenor saxophonist/composer Charlie Rouse. This specific rhythm melody features eighth notes, as you'll see by examining the music on the next page. Actually, the melody is almost all eighth notes, except for 6 downbeat quarter notes.

1 My Little Sherri ♩= *ca.* 118
trumpet melody

Listen to **track 1** of the accompanying CD. You'll immediately notice that the 4 measure rhythm section introduction sets up a strong triplet feeling ♪♪♪ (3). The drummer plays triplets and the bass and piano punctuate with what is known as a "Charleston" figure, usually written: ♩. 𝄾 ♪. With a constant stream of triplets from the drums, the piano and bass are actually playing ♩. 𝄾 𝄾 ♪ (3), so their patterns will fit into the drummer's eighth note triplet groove. The tempo of track 1 is ♩= *ca.* 118, a medium slow swing tempo, so you can easily hear and feel the triplet groove. The melody is played with a triplet-eighth note feeling.

This is the same triplet eighth note groove that lyricist/singer Ben Sidran used when he recorded his lyric version, except he "heard" the song

My Little Sherri

Music by Charlie Rouse
Lyric by Ben Sidran

Instrumentally known as "Little Sherri"

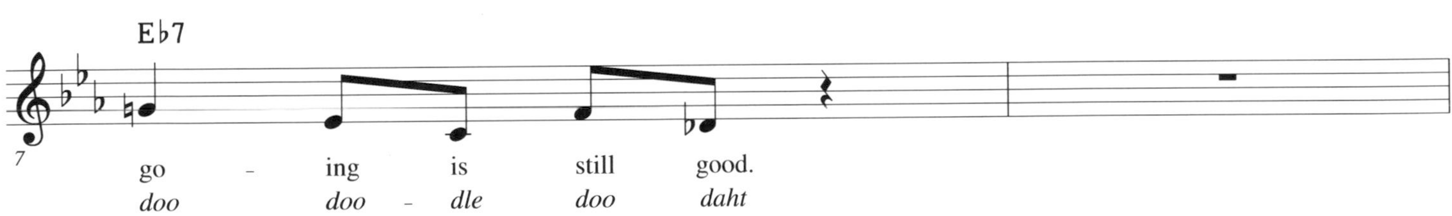

at a faster tempo (♩= *ca.* 188). The following examples will help you understand some of the effects of different tempos, so you'll learn to "hear" the right tempo for your own version. The vocal and instrumental discography on page 52 lists other recordings of the songs in this workshop—listen to as many as you can.

Play **track 1** through several times, listening to the melody. Once you have the melody in your ear, sing along with the trumpet. It may help, the first few times, to sing syllables instead of the lyric, so you can focus on the melody and the rhythm. Sample syllables are shown under the lyric in italics, or you can make up your own syllables. Also, independent of the recording, if you have a keyboard, try playing the melody yourself to help you get the intervals in your ear. When you sing along with the trumpet, you should try to blend with the trumpet both melodically and rhythmically, to achieve a real unison sound. This is what two horn players would try to achieve, when playing the melody together.

❷ My Little Sherri ♩= *ca.* 118
trumpet melody and vocal syllables

In **track 2** the trumpet melody is joined by a vocalist, Angela DeNiro, singing her own syllables. Practice singing along, concentrating on the intervals and the triplet eighth feeling.

❸ My Little Sherri ♩= *ca.* 118
rhythm section alone: you sing!

Track 3 features the rhythm section alone. The piano plays your first note at the beginning of the track. Sing along with the rhythm section using syllables to help you become more comfortable with the melody, phrasing and tempo. Then try to sing the lyric along with track 3 in the triplet-style eighth note phrasing the rhythm section is playing and make your performance convincing.

Now we'd like to change the feel of ***My Little Sherri*** and explore several different tempos with the CD examples. As you listen and sing along, try to become conscious of the subtle differences in phrasing between each tempo. You'll find that the song assumes a new identity with each new tempo. Discover which one you like best, which tempo fits best with the way *you* hear the melody. Notice that as the tempos get faster, the eighth notes will tend to become more even.

For the following examples, you can use the same procedure as with tracks 1-3: listen to the melody, then sing along. Try to become aware of phrasing differences while matching your phrasing to the melody. Then experiment with each new tempo by singing with the rhythm section.

❹ My Little Sherri ♩= *ca.* 122
trumpet melody

Track 4: now we'll raise the tempo slightly, change the "feel" and switch to a 2 measure introduction. The bass is going to "walk" (play quarter notes) and the drummer will change to sticks and play what we call "time" on the cymbals (also emphasizing the quarter note pulse). Listen to the trumpet playing the melody at ♩= 122, then sing syllables along with the trumpet as you try to match the phrasing.

With this new feeling in the rhythm section, notice how the trumpet takes more liberties phrasing the eighth notes. Some are still part of triplets (♪♪♪), while others become more even eighth notes. Instrumentalists can't tell their story with words; in order to make the melody live and breathe they employ subtle articulation and phrasing nuances. Vocalists also rely on phrasing, articulation and tone to tell a convincing story, and they must add an additional element: the lyric. The vocalist's phrasing has to work on two levels; (1) the melodic and rhythmic phrasing must be convincing, like the instrumentalist's, and (2) the lyric must also tell an emotionally convincing story.

5 My Little Sherri ♩ = *ca.* 122
Angela sings the lyric

Listen to how Angela sings the lyric at this same tempo in **track 5**. At this relatively slow tempo, she's keeping a real swinging feeling going, with mostly triplet eighth note phrasing, in contrast to the slightly more even eighth note approach by the trumpet in track 4. Remember, there is no rule: each performance has to have its own validity.

6 My Little Sherri ♩ = *ca.* 122
rhythm section alone: you sing!

You get your chance to sing with the rhythm section in **track 6**. How do you hear the song at this tempo? Do you still hear it with swing eighths, or do you hear the eighth notes more even at times?

7 My Little Sherri ♩ = *ca.* 140
trumpet melody

8 My Little Sherri ♩ = *ca.* 140
vocal syllables

9 My Little Sherri ♩ = *ca.* 140
rhythm section alone: you sing!

Listen to the trumpet play **track 7** (♩ = *ca.* 140), then sing along. If you try to match the trumpet's phrasing, you'll be more aware of the subtle differences between his even eighth note phrasing and swing eighth note phrasing.

In **track 8** you can hear Angela sing syllables along with the rhythm section. Listen to the variety of syllables she uses and how they affect her articulation. Try it on your own (**track 9**).

10 My Little Sherri ♩ = *ca.* 160
trumpet melody

11 My Little Sherri ♩ = *ca.* 160
rhythm section alone: you sing!

Track 10: at ♩ = *ca.* 160, listen again for swing eighths and more even eighths. Try it with the rhythm section alone (**track 11**).

12 My Little Sherri ♩ = *ca.* 178
trumpet melody

13 My Little Sherri ♩ = *ca.* 178
hear the lyric

14 My Little Sherri ♩ = *ca.* 178
rhythm section alone: you sing!

To set up faster tempos, we've lengthened the introduction to 4 measures:

♩ = *ca.* 178

track 12: trumpet melody with the rhythm section

track 13: Angela sings the lyric with the rhythm section

track 14: your chance to sing with the rhythm section

15 My Little Sherri ♩ = *ca.* 190
trumpet melody

16 My Little Sherri ♩ = *ca.* 190
rhythm section alone: you sing!

In **track 15** (♩ = *ca.* 190) can you identify more even eighth notes in the trumpet melody at this tempo? **Track 16**: can you make this tempo comfortable for your own version?

17 My Little Sherri ♩ = *ca.* 190
trumpet melody Charleston

18 My Little Sherri ♩ = *ca.* 190
hear the lyric Charleston

19 My Little Sherri ♩ = *ca.* 190
rhythm section alone: you sing! Charleston

Kevin Mahogany recorded this song at approximately ♩ = 198, and he kept the Charleston feel going. Listen to how the trumpet approaches the Charleston feel in **track 17**, then sing along. Notice that the triplet eighth note feeling predominates. Hear Angela's version in **track 18**, then try it yourself with the rhythm section in **track 19**.

My Little Sherri is a good song to explore eighth note phrasing because it contains many different combinations of eighth notes, from a 2-eighth-note group to 8 consecutive eighth notes. The melody line contains twisting and turning patterns of eighth notes that either land on downbeats or end syncopated (two eighth notes followed by a rest). The melody works well in a variety of tempos and styles, as the previous examples demonstrate.

20 My Little Sherri ♩ = 160
vocal beat box and lyric

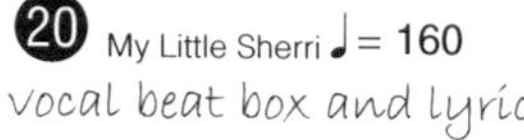

What would happen if we changed the eighth note feeling of this song entirely, from swing eighth notes to even eighth notes? Even eighth note phrasing is widely used in many styles of today's popular music and it could be effective in ***My Little Sherri*** as well. With all the eighth notes even, it takes on a completely different character. Listen to Akil Dasan's vocal beat box rhythm background with his overdubbed rap of the lyric (**track 20**). Akil sets up the rap with an 8 measure introduction, creating all the rhythm sounds simultaneously.

To summarize: As you evaluate songs you want to perform and develop arrangement concepts for your performances, first decide on the tempo and style you want. The tempo you choose will affect the way you and your accompanists think about and phrase eighth notes. Once you understand how you want to present the song, explain your approach to your rhythm section, since their accompaniment style must compliment your interpretation.

It's important to listen to many different jazz artists on recordings and in live performances so you can become aware of the many subtle differences in the way they approach eighth notes. Once you recognize their phrasing concepts, you can incorporate them into your own performances. Listen to instrumentalists and vocalists: you can learn from both.

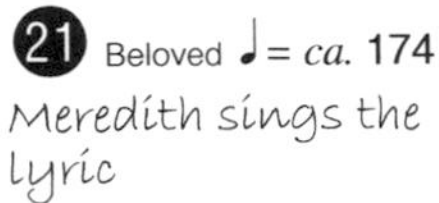

Meredith sings the lyric

Sometimes melodic even eighth notes are called for in a jazz song that has a seemingly contradictory tempo indication, like medium swing. Listen to **track 21**, an excerpt from Meredith d'Ambrosio's recording of ***Beloved***.

Meredith has a low voice and sings ***Beloved*** in the key of F. Clifford Brown wrote the original song in E♭ concert. Since he was a trumpet player, he played the melody in the key of F. Meredith enjoys the fact that she sings the melody in Clifford's key. The music example below and on tracks 22 and 23 are in B♭.

Sung by Meredith d'Ambrosio on Love Is For The Birds (Sunnyside SSC 1101D)

Beloved

Instrumentally known as "Daahoud"

Music by Clifford Brown
Lyric by Meredith d'Ambrosio

Medium swing

F7♯5(♯9) | (A) B♭m7 E♭7 A♭m7 | D♭7 | G♭maj7

When you ap-peared on the scene, ___ sud-den-ly I did-n't know what to say,

The rhythm section figures and the rhythm section feeling for this song is swing, but the melody should be phrased as even eighths. ***Beloved*** is Meredith d'Ambrosio's lyric to legendary trumpeter Clifford Brown's important jazz standard ***Daahoud***, originally written and recorded by Clifford in 1956. ***Daahoud*** is a classic jazz standard and is well known in jazz circles. Clifford always played the melody as even eighths. Meredith echoes Clifford Brown's original phrasing, as would most jazz musicians.

Clifford played ***Daahoud*** up tempo, with lots of energy. His tempo is much too fast for a lyric version. Meredith sings it in a medium swing tempo (♩ = *ca.* 174). The slower tempo allows the lyric to be clearly articulated. If you try to sing ***Beloved*** too fast, with all those eighth notes, the lyric won't be understood. Always keep good diction and clear articulation in mind when choosing a tempo.

22 Beloved ♩= *ca.* 194
trumpet melody

23 Beloved ♩= *ca.* 194
rhythm section alone: you sing!

Faster tempos are challenging: on **track 22**, listen to the trumpet play this excerpt at ♩ = *ca.* 194. On **track 23**, sing the opening two phases of ***Beloved*** at the same tempo. How does this tempo work for you?

Look again at ***My Little Sherri*** on page 7. Like ***Beloved***, it also starts with an eighth note rest followed by 7 eighth notes, but the two songs phrase the melodic eighth notes very differently.

The next song illustrates another type of eighth note phrasing. We call it phrasing eighth notes in a groove. Pianist Bertha Hope's composition ***You Know Who!*** is a great example of a song built on a groove. The eighth note phrasing groove is set up in the first measure of the introduction and must be maintained by the rhythm section throughout the Ⓐ section, as shown in the example. The groove starts as a 4 eighth note bass line, then adds an eighth note pickup to become a 5 eighth note phrase.

24 You Know Who! ♩= *ca.* 112
flugelhorn melody

Listen to **track 24** and notice how the flugelhorn plays the melody with the "groove feel" set up by the rhythm section. When everyone phrases a groove song together it really works. Try singing along with the flugelhorn, getting yourself synchronized with the groove.

25 You Know Who! ♩= *ca.* 112
rhythm section alone: you sing!

Sing along with **track 25**, without the flugelhorn, putting yourself into the groove with the rhythm section.

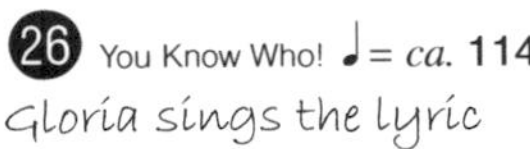
You Know Who! ♩ = *ca.* 114
Gloria sings the lyric

The addition of lyrics to a melody means you have a story to tell, as well as a melody to sing. This story can certainly be told "inside the groove," but notice how Gloria Cooper uses subtle inflections on her recording of ***You Know Who!*** to emphasize her version of the story (**track 26**). Gloria sings in Gm, down a whole step from the music shown below. On this recording, Gloria is the vocalist and also the pianist. She wanted to emphasize "and blue" in measure 1 and "so tough!" in measure 6, so she lays back on these words, singing them a little later and therefore giving them more emphasis. In the example below look at measures 1 and 6. The arrows are under the words which she delayed slightly. Listen to how her piano playing stays right in the groove with the rhythm section. Obviously she feels where the groove is, and she's still able to take the liberties necessary to express her viewpoint of the story vocally.

As sung by Gloria Cooper on Day By Day (GAC Music GAC 1001)

You Know Who!

Music and Lyric by
Bertha Hope

Medium groove

Intro

Am F13(♯11) Am F13(♯11)

rhythm section *mf*

melody

When you are

rhythm section *simile* intro

(A) Am F13(♯11) Am F13(♯11) Am F13(♯11)

lone - ly and blue, don't know what to do, cry a - while.

Am F13(♯11) Am F13(♯11) Am F13(♯11)

When things are look - in' rough, and you're not so tough,

Am F13(♯11) Am F13(♯11)

sigh a - while.

Most performances with a group require a count off to lock the whole ensemble into the tempo. You should first get the tempo in your head, then count it off. A discreet count off, unobtrusive to the audience, works best. Make sure you have contact with all your musicians so they hear (or see) your count off. If you are performing with just a single accompanist, don't let him or her set the tempo with an introduction on their own. You're the one who needs to make sure the tempo is right for your performance of the lyric. This method will work great for ***My Little Sherri*** and ***You Know Who!***, since those songs are set up with intros.

The vocalist can't count off in our example of ***Beloved***. It starts with a one chord introduction on the and-of-4, and the melody comes right in with all those eighth notes: it's too cumbersome for the vocalist to also count off. In situations like that, assign the count off to one of your band members. Make sure he or she knows the tempo you want. Snap your fingers on 2 and 4 for a couple of measures or give them some other type of preliminary count, then let them count off.

27 Sweet And True ♩= *ca.* 104
cymbal rhythm

Before hearing the next song, ***Sweet And True***, listen to and examine the cymbal pattern below (**track 27**).

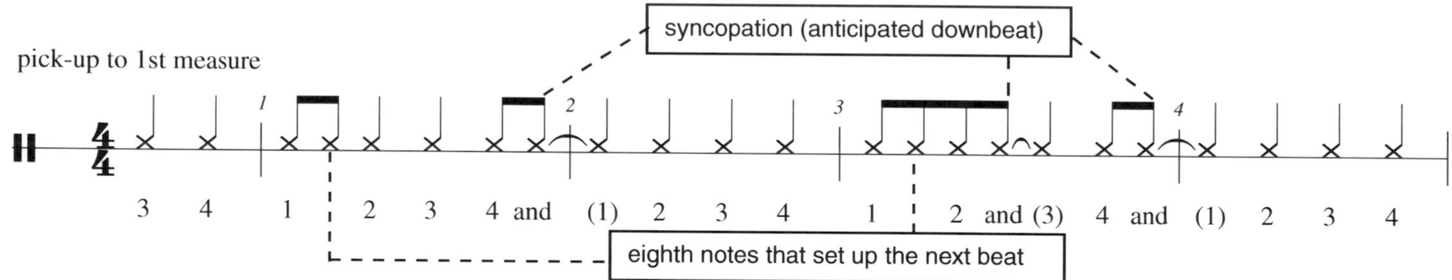

The drummer is keeping the quarter note pulse going (playing on each beat) except for the 1st beats of measures 2 and 4 and the 3rd beat of measure 3, where the downbeats are anticipated as part of a syncopated eighth note figure. The syncopations must have the right feeling, otherwise you will have trouble picking up the pulse again on the 2nd beat of measures 2 and 4 and 4th beat of measure 3. The eighth notes between the 1st and 2nd beats of measures 1 and 3 have a different function. They have to set up the next beat. These notes can make or break the swing feeling.

28 Sweet And True ♩= *ca.* 104
the first 4 measures only

Now listen to the first 4 measures of ***Sweet and True*** on **track 28**. The melody and rhythm section phrases must flow together seamlessly, although they are played by different musicians. Everyone must feel the pulse together and phrase together. The melody's eighth note phrasing has to help set up the rhythm section entrance.

Listen to track 28 again, looking at the cymbal pattern. Hear how the melody and rhythm phrases fit into the cymbal pattern.

Examine the music for these 4 measures below. The curved arrows point out critical eighth note movement.

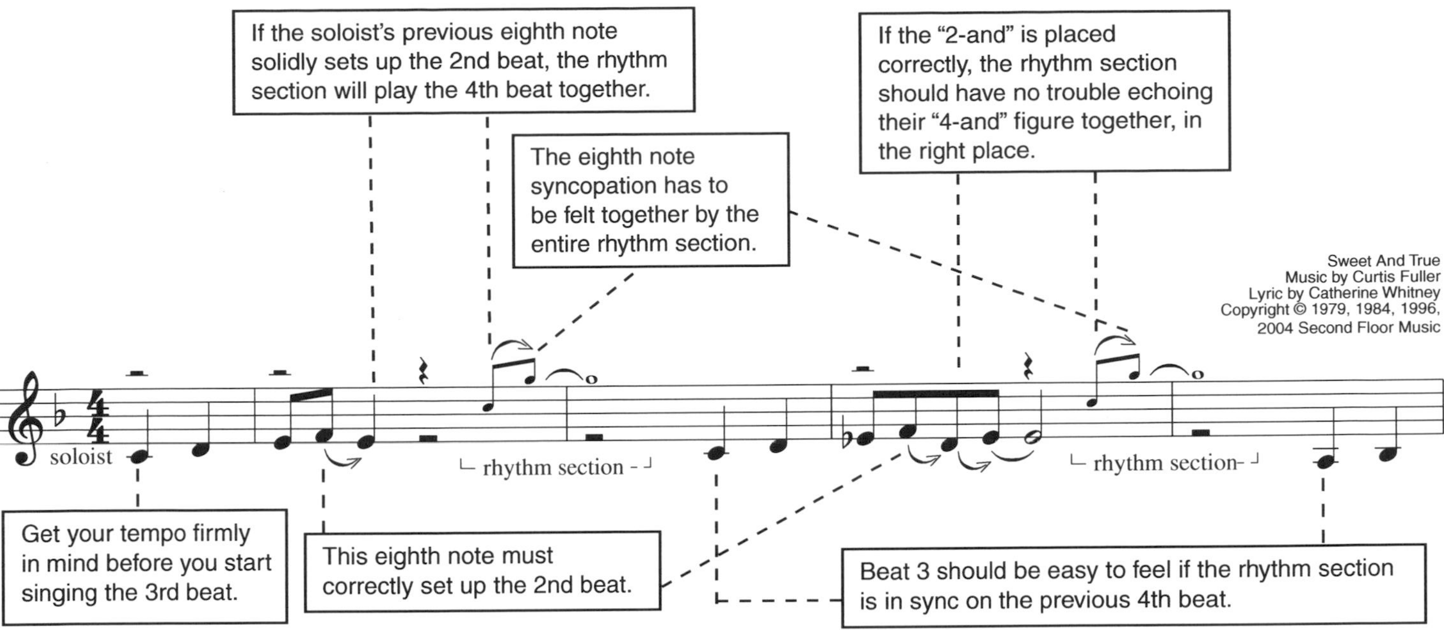

The cymbal pattern is easier to play than the song. The drummer, playing the cymbal line in track 27, can hold everything together with ease, because he also *plays* the 3rd beat of measure 1 and the 2nd beat of measures 2 and 4. In performing the song, no one plays those beats. Everyone has to *feel* them together.

Sweet And True was conceived and recorded instrumentally by renowned trombonist/composer Curtis Fuller as a "no introduction" song. This isn't to say that you couldn't create an introduction to set up the melody for your own vocal arrangement. However, an introduction is not necessary.

We recommend that you first try this song with your group without an introduction. In fact, we don't even want you or anyone in your group to count off. You must set up the band yourself with the first 5 notes. Just make sure, before starting to sing, that you have your tempo clearly in your head. You and all the members of your ensemble can gain valuable group phrasing experience from trying this no-count-off approach. It's also very dramatic if you make the first entrance alone, with no visible count off.

29 30 Sweet And True ♩= *ca.* 104
flugelhorn melody

Learn the melody first by singing along with the flugelhorn on **track 29** and **track 30** (see the melody on the following page).

Tracks 29 and 30 also provide an opportunity to examine different styles of accompaniment. The flugelhorn plays the melody as written in both tracks, but the pianist approaches them differently.

29 Sweet And True ♩= *ca.* 104
flugelhorn melody, piano playing figures

In **track 29**, the pianist plays all the figures with the flugelhorn: the "and" of 2 in measures 5 and 7 and the new chords that lead into measures 10, 11, 12 and 13. This approach gives good support to the melody, and you may prefer it behind your vocal.

30 Sweet And True ♩= *ca.* 104
flugelhorn melody, piano not playing figures

However, the pianist could avoid playing most or all of the phrases with the melody, as in **track 30**. This will give the pianist more creative space and it will also let the soloist feel freer to express the melody. Notice the chord symbols positioned at the end of measures 9, 10, 11 and 12. The syncopated melody notes under the chord symbols are members of the new chords, not the old chords, therefore the chord symbols are placed above the changing harmonic notes. This chord symbol placement doesn't mean that everyone has to syncopate the rhythm accordingly. Notice that the bassist primarily plays downbeats while the pianist syncopates with the melody in track 29.

One basic role of the bassist is to make sure that the tempo doesn't creep up or down. The bass player can make sure the tempo stays steady by maintaining a strong 2-feel downbeat presence as opposed to always syncopating with the piano at the end of the measure. Notice that the drummer plays simply, just concentrating on keeping the "time" swinging and flowing.

31 Sweet And True ♩= *ca.* 130
Gloria sings the lyric

Unfortunately this is a song that doesn't work in a background-minus-the-melody format, so there is no rhythm section alone track on the CD. However, here's another interpretation of the melody to listen to and to look at. **Track 31** is an excerpt of Gloria Cooper's recording of ***Sweet And True***, and the music example below is a transcription of how Gloria interpreted the melody on that recorded performance. Gloria hears some of the phrases less syncopated (measures 5, 11-12) at her faster tempo. Her phrasing of "just let it go," is conversational, and she sings "it" just a little sooner than the triplet would indicate.

Sweet and True, like most songs, can be performed at different tempos. Don, on flugelhorn, hears the song in a medium slow groove. He plays tracks 29 and 30 at ♩ = *ca.* 104. Gloria's recording is faster, with more energy, a medium swing tempo (♩ = *ca.* 130). When composer/trombonist Curtis Fuller recorded the composition instrumentally with Kai Winding (two trombones) under the instrumental title of ***Sweetness***, the tempo was a much slower groove, ♩ = *ca.* 98; when he recorded it with tenor saxophonist Benny Golson, the tempo was ♩ = *ca.* 124.

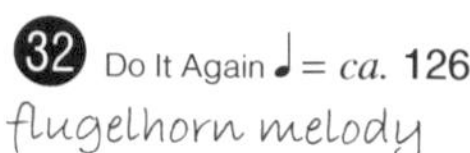

If you have a drummer in your rhythm section, often it's his or her responsibility to set up the first melodic entrance. In the arrangement of ***Do It Again*** **(track 32)**, listen to how the drummer sets up the 2 measure rhythm section introduction.

You could try a different approach without an introduction by establishing a count off yourself, singing the vocal pickup solo (*Oh*), then have the rhythm section start swinging behind you right at Ⓐ.

The song's basic melodic pattern should be familiar to you by now (at Ⓐ: 4 eighth notes tied into the 3rd beat). It's a new look at the "groove" pattern from ***You Know Who!*** and a pattern that is also used 6 times in the ***Sweet And True*** example. In ***Do It Again*** the energy is different. It's all about syncopations and how the eighth notes set them up. In the first ending, the driving 4 note rhythm figure cleverly shifts to the 4th beat and continues across the bar line, emphasizing the syncopation in a different way. This composition was written for the premiere jazz drummer Arthur Taylor ("A.T." as he was affectionately known), and he used it as his theme song. He loved its driving, swinging feel.

Tracks 32-45 provide several tempos for experimentation. As in ***My Little Sherri***, notice how some of the melody eighth notes can become more even as the tempos get faster. However, if you sing even eighths you must still feel the syncopations with everyone else.

33 Do It Again ♩ = *ca.* 126
vocal syllables
34 Do It Again ♩ = *ca.* 126
rhythm section alone: you sing!

♩ = *ca.* 126
track 33 Angela sings syllables
track 34 your chance to sing with the rhythm section

35 Do It Again ♩ = *ca.* 138
flugelhorn melody
36 Do It Again ♩ = *ca.* 138
hear the lyric
37 Do It Again ♩ = *ca.* 138
rhythm section alone: you sing!

♩ = *ca.* 138
track 35 flugelhorn melody with the rhythm section
track 36 Angela sings the lyric with the rhythm section
track 37 your chance to sing with the rhythm section

38 Do It Again ♩ = *ca.* 152
flugelhorn melody
39 Do It Again ♩ = *ca.* 152
hear the lyric
40 Do It Again ♩ = *ca.* 152
rhythm section alone: you sing!

♩ = *ca.* 152
track 38 flugelhorn melody with the rhythm section
track 39 Angela sings the lyric with the rhythm section
track 40 your chance to sing with the rhythm section

41 Do It Again ♩ = *ca.* 172
flugelhorn melody
42 Do It Again ♩ = *ca.* 172
flugelhorn melody and vocal syllables
43 Do It Again ♩ = *ca.* 172
duo: flugelhorn and vocal syllables only
44 Do It Again ♩ = *ca.* 172
hear the lyric
45 Do It Again ♩ = *ca.* 172
rhythm section alone: you sing!

♩ = *ca.* 172
track 41 flugelhorn melody with the rhythm section
track 42 flugelhorn melody, vocal syllables and rhythm

track 43 a duo: flugelhorn melody and vocal syllables
Practicing duo with no rhythm section is very demanding but very rewarding when everything is in sync and in tune.

track 44 Angela sings the lyric with the rhythm section
track 45 your chance to sing with the rhythm section

To summarize: All the songs we have discussed so far have sections that require *specific rhythm phrasing*. This means that the rhythmic content of these melody sections is important to the song. If the rhythm isn't closely observed, the song looses its identity. The eighth notes within these sections can be phrased differently, depending on style and tempo. We've heard varying degrees of "swing" eighth notes in ***My Little Sherri***, even eighth notes in ***Beloved***, eighth notes that fit into a rhythm section groove (***You Know Who!***), eighth notes that set up downbeats (***Sweet And True***) or set up syncopations (***Sweet And True*** and ***Do It Again***). As we've seen, the tempo you choose can affect your eighth note phrasing. At faster tempos eighth notes can generally be sung more evenly, for example. The accompaniment instruments must agree on how to phrase the eighth notes, as well. If it is a groove song, your eighth notes have to work with the groove played by the accompanying instruments. If you have a good swinging rhythm section, follow their lead.

Specific Rhythm Figures

There's one more type of specific rhythm phrase where the melody and the rhythms coincide. When playing specific rhythm figures, the entire ensemble has to feel and play all the rhythms and notes of the section together or it won't work.

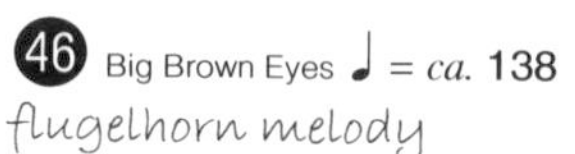

46 Big Brown Eyes ♩ = *ca.* 138
flugelhorn melody

47 Big Brown Eyes ♩ = *ca.* 138
hear the lyric

48 Big Brown Eyes ♩ = *ca.* 138
rhythm section alone: you sing!

Look at the next example, ***Big Brown Eyes***, and listen to **track 46.** Obviously, having a good swinging drummer to set up the specific rhythm figures is very helpful in getting everyone to feel all the entrances together. Angela sings the lyric on **track 47**.

This song can be performed in a variety of tempos. At what tempo do you hear it? On tracks 46 and 47 it is performed at ♩ = *ca.* 138. Try it yourself at that tempo (**track 48**).

49 Big Brown Eyes ♩ = *ca.* 166
flugelhorn melody

50 Big Brown Eyes ♩ = *ca.* 166
hear the lyric

51 Big Brown Eyes ♩ = *ca.* 166
rhythm section alone: you sing!

Now try it a little faster, with the drummer on sticks. The flugelhorn plays the melody in **track 49** at ♩ = *ca.* 166. In **track 50** you can hear the melody sung. Try it yourself (**track 51**). Does this tempo work for you?

Before you count off any song you are about to perform, think carefully about the tempo. Make sure you have the right tempo in mind for your performance and communicate the tempo to the musicians in your group.

Big Brown Eyes

Instrumentally known as "Glo's Theme"

Music by Tommy Turrentine
Lyric by L. Aziza Miller

Medium swing

Drums
A
Dmll G9(13) Cmaj7
Big brown eyes,
big brown eyes,
Drums or instrumental fill
Ebmll Ab9(13) Dbmaj7
let me know,
tell me, please,

(Dbmaj7)
fill
Emll A9(13) Dmaj7
should I stay
are you play - ing
fill
Ebmll
or

1.
Dmll G9(13) Emll Ebmll
should I go? ___ Hey,

2.
Dmll G9(13) Cmaj7
games with me?

Open Phrasing

Exploring different musical environments

The other end of the spectrum from specific rhythm phrasing is what we call **open phrasing**, where the rhythmic flow of the melody is determined by the vocalist's phrasing. The notated rhythm is just a general guide. The vocalist will shape the melody rhythmically using the decided-upon tempo, style and instrumentation (accompaniment) as a guide. Open phrasing sections should be easily recognizable because the rhythmic notation of the melody is very simple, using little or no syncopation. Look at the opening section of the ***I'm Movin' On*** lead sheet as it appears in the ***Sing JAZZ!*** songbook.

Sing the lyric with the rhythms notated in the example above to get the general flow of the music and to learn the melody. This song is perfect for exploring creative interpretations, as you'll see in the following pages.

In preparing for this publication, we went into the recording studio with lyricist/vocalist Judy Niemack, guitarist Jeanfrançois Prins and our New York rhythm section. We met in Rudy Van Gelder's legendary Englewood Cliffs studio, where Judy had dreamt of recording. We knew ***I'm Movin' On*** would be perfect for explaining open phrasing, and the circumstances would encourage creative results from everyone as we explored different musical environments for this song. The following printed and audio examples reflect the variations and changes that occurred as the accompaniment "feels" and tempos changed from version to version. You'll hear and see what happens to the music as the musicians spontaneously react to various suggestions. It's interesting to observe how different the written transcriptions of Judy's performances look on paper as compared to the original lead sheet of ***I'm Movin' On***.

The first goal was to get a good basic recording the way Judy wanted to perform the song. However, we asked her not to deviate from the melody, to limit her improvisations to variations in rhythm and phrasing. First, she explained the fundamentals of how she wanted to approach the song. After a 2-against-3 introduction, she wanted the group to flow into an open 1-feel so she could freely interpret the melody. It was decided that the piano would drop out after the introduction, leaving the guitar to supply the harmonic framework. When the melody returned, after a guitar solo, the piano would take over the role of predominant accompanist.

We've placed extra CD track numbers at various places in the following audio tracks so you can easily locate or repeat sections. The track number is placed in the music notation where the tracks begin in order to help you immediately locate certain outlined sections for practice or listening purposes. On Judy's vocal interpretation tracks, her entrances are preceded by a rhythm section introduction to set the style and mood. If you want to hear Judy's interpretations only, or compare her approach to different styles, listen to tracks 52, 53, 54, 56, 58, 60, 63, 65 and 67. We've also marked the rhythm section alone tracks where you can experiment with your own interpretations. There's usually a 2 measure introduction to set up your entrance (for example, track 55 starts 2 measures before (3) on page 25). For those rhythm section tracks, listen to tracks 55, 57, 59, 61, 64, 66 and 68. You can use your CD player's repeat and programming functions for further experimentation.

The music notation for the example on page 23 and all the following examples of ***I'm Movin' On*** is deliberately complicated and non-conventional, in order to illustrate and help you analyze important nuances in Judy's performances. You'll see and hear, for example, that the way words end is as important as how they begin. Often, there is no rhythmic notation in the staff for the end of a word, instead there's just a hyphen leading to the letter or syllable which ends the word. This positional approximation of the enunciation of word endings will help you listen for them.

(52) I'm Movin' On ♩ = *ca.* 176
Judy sings the (A) melody, then the track fades out

(53) I'm Movin' On
fades in after guitar solo, for Judy's out chorus (A^2)

For the purposes of this demonstration, you will hear Judy sing two (A) sections. See the following page of music, and listen to **track 52** (A^1) and **track 53** (A^2) in sequence. Compare the melody notes of the lead sheet melody on page 21 with the notes Judy sings when she introduces the melody for the first time at (A^1) on page 23. The notes are the same, but

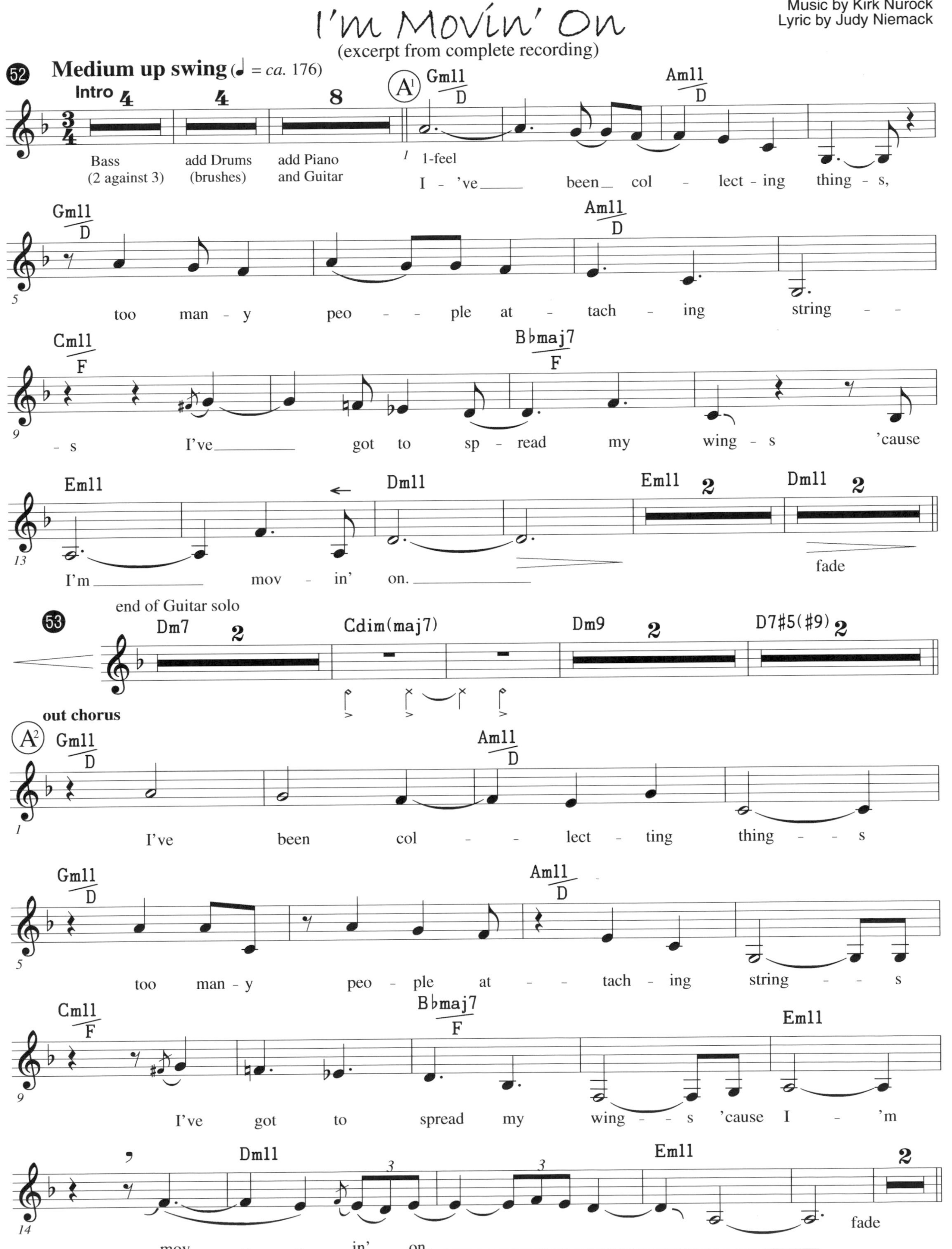
I'm Movin' On
(excerpt from complete recording)
Music by Kirk Nurock
Lyric by Judy Niemack
52
Medium up swing (♩ = ca. 176)
Intro
Bass (2 against 3)
add Drums (brushes)
add Piano and Guitar
A1
1-feel
Gm11/D
Am11/D
I - 've been col - lect - ing thing - s,
too man - y peo - - - ple at - tach - ing string - - - s
Cm11/F
B♭maj7/F
I've got to sp - read my wing - s 'cause
Em11
Dm11
I'm mov - in' on.
fade
53
end of Guitar solo
Dm7
Cdim(maj7)
Dm9
D7♯5(♯9)
out chorus
A2
I've been col - - - lect - ting thing - - - s
too man - y peo - ple at - - - tach - ing string - - - s
I've got to spread my wing - - s 'cause I - 'm
mov - - - in' on.
fade

the rhythmic flow is different. In the transcriptions we've used symbols to indicate some of her subtle rhythmic shifts. For example, an arrow over a note means the note is sung a little before (←) or after (→) the notated rhythm.

Often an artist will embellish or change melody notes in re-telling the story for a second time when the melody is restated for the out chorus, as in Ⓐ^{2} (page 23). This is an improvisatory technique that most jazz artists use. Note Judy's "new" notes in measures 3, 4 and 5 of Ⓐ^{2} (track 53, page 23). Also, this time (Ⓐ^{2} track 53) she sings the optional melody notes found in measures 11 and 12 of the original lead sheet. Then she elongates the "F" melody note in measure 14 and creates a different way to end the phrase, reversing the roles of the last two melody notes.

Once we finished recording a complete take to Judy's specifications, we started to experiment with some of her ideas, and add some of our own, in order to try alternate ways to approach this song. We knew that as we suggested tempo and background changes, Judy would come up with new phrasing approaches for the melody. The following examples detail some of the things we learned from this musical adventure.

2-against-3

Since Judy wanted a nice open 1-feel under the melody for her basic version, for our first variation we decided to use her 2-against-3 introduction idea under the melody. The bass player's role is crucial in creating new musical environments. The bass figure that sets the mood in each new environment will be shown first (see the figure below).

Medium up swing (♩ = *ca.* 178)

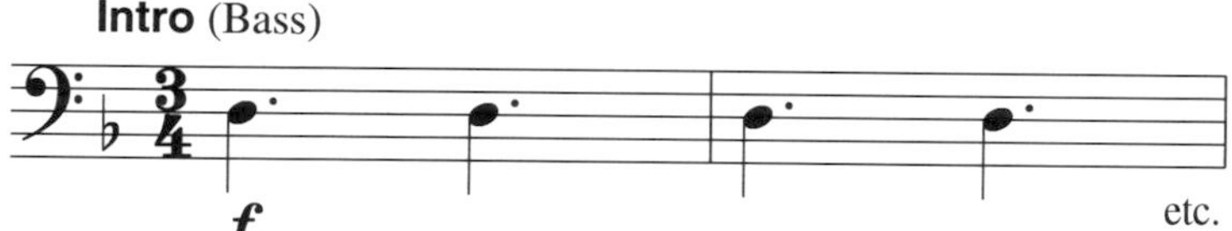

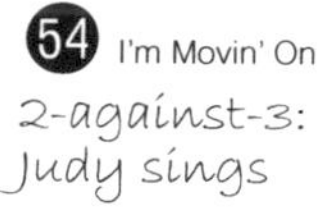

54 I'm Movin' On
2-against-3: Judy sings

55 I'm Movin' On
rhythm section alone: you sing!

Listen to what the musicians came up with on **track 54** and examine the music notation on page 25. Judy sings the 20-bar Ⓐ section (the melody) twice (① and ②). On the CD this is immediately followed by 4 more Ⓐ sections without Judy (**track 55:** ③, ④, ⑤ and ⑥), so you can try your own ideas with the rhythm section. The same procedure is followed for all the other ***I'm Movin' On*** examples.

With the steady dotted-quarter-note pulse under her, we loved Judy's opening phrase as she sang half notes over the bass's dotted quarter notes (① track 54). At ② she returns to a solid 3/4 feel over the 2-against-3 bass figure.

The notation ⌐ *4:3* ¬ indicates that Judy is feeling 4-against-3, which further subdivides the 2-against-3 line of the bass.

Medium up swing (♩ = ca. 178) 2-against-3
I'm Movin' On
Music by Kirk Nurock
Lyric by Judy Niemack
54
Intro
rhythm section
Gm11/D
Am11/D
I've been col - lect - ing thing - - s,
too man - y peo - ple at - tach - ing string - - - s,
Cm11/F
B♭maj7/F
I've got to spread my wing - - s 'cause
Em11
Dm11
I'm mov - in' on.
I've been col - lect - ing thing - - s
4:3
too man - y peo - ple at - tach - ing string - - - s,
I've got to spread my wing - - s 'cause
I'm mov - in' on.
55
fade

Walking bass, drums (brushes)

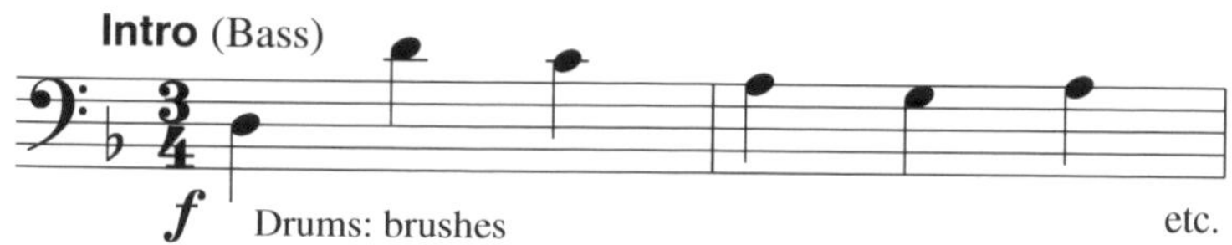

56 I'm Movin' On
walking bass, drums (brushes): Judy sings

57 I'm Movin' On
rhythm section alone: you sing!

Having explored a 2-against-3 feel and a 1-feel, we wanted to see how Judy would phrase the melody if the bass walked. We recorded two takes, the first with drums playing brushes (**tracks 56-57**), the second with drums using sticks (**tracks 58-59**, pages 28-29).

With the bass walking, Judy starts by singing 2-against-3.

Listen to Judy's dynamic shaping. Some of her more obvious dynamics are notated with crescendos and decrescendos (see (1) measures 15 through 18), but there are many more dynamic inflections you should listen for in her singing.

Judy usually delays the melody of measure 9 ("I've"), but this time she anticipates it (starting in measure 8 of (1), track 56).

Listen for the subtle nuances and changes that take place in Judy's phrasing as related to the accompaniment. Communication and response between all the musicians is vital in developing a balanced, unified and convincing performance of any song.

I'm Movin' On
Music by Kirk Nurock
Lyric by Judy Niemack

Medium up swing (♩ = *ca.* 202) walking Bass (Drums: brushes)

56

Intro 8 — rhythm section

(1) Gm11/D Am11/D

I've been col - lect - ing thing - - s,

Gm11/D Am11/D

too man - y peo - ple at - tach - ing strings, I' -

Cm11/F B♭maj7/F

- - 've got to spread my wing - - - - s

Em11 Dm11 Em11 Dm11 2

'cause I'm mov - in' on.

(2) Gm11/D Am11/D

I've been col - lec - ting thing - s

Gm11/D Am11/D

too man - y peo - ple at - tach - ing string - -

Cm11/F B♭maj7/F

- s I got - ta spread my wings 'cause

Em11 Dm11 Em11

I'm mov - in' on.

57

Dm11 2 (3) 20 (4) 20 (5) 20 (6) 20

fade

Walking bass, drums (sticks)

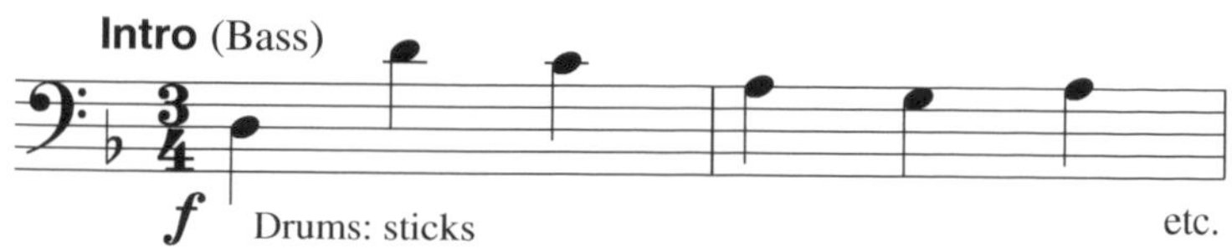

58 I'm Movin' On
walking bass, drums (sticks): Judy sings

59 I'm Movin' On
rhythm section alone: you sing!

For the second walking bass example the drums changed to sticks (**tracks 58-59**). Judy starts ① with the same half note pulses that she interjected against the dotted quarter note pulses in the previous 2-against-3 example (track 54, page 25), but this time she comes out of the half notes into the quarter note pulses of the bass. In track 54, interestingly, she came out of the half note pulses into the dotted quarter note pulses of the bass.

Judy's phrases that appear similar in notation from example to example may sound entirely different because of their varying background treatments. For example, Judy likes the 2-against-3 feeling and consecutive half note pulses against 3/4. At Ⓐ² in track 53 (page 23) her half note pulses start on the 2nd beat. In track 54 ① (page 25) the half note pulses start on the 1st beat, as they do in ① of track 58 (page 29).

In ② of track 58, Judy delays her entrance then sings quarter notes with the bass player for the first three melody notes.

Notice how Judy changes the inflections of words from arrangement to arrangement. We hear some ascending and descending slides on certain words as Judy chooses to emphasize differing emotions on particular phrases or words.

In track 58 she stretches out the "I'm movin' on" phrase (measure 14 through 20 of ①. Contrast that approach with measures 14-20 of ②. Compare measure 12 ① "'cause" to measure 13 ② "'cause."

Medium up swing (♩ = ca. 208) walking Bass (Drums: sticks)
I'm Movin' On
Music by Kirk Nurock
Lyric by Judy Niemack
58
Intro 8
rhythm section
Gm11/D Am11/D Cm11/F B♭maj7/F Em11 Dm11
I've been col - lec - ting thing - - - s,
too man - y peo - ple at - tach - ing string - - - - s I got - ta spread my wing - - s 'cause I - 'm
mov - in' on.
I - 've been col - lec - ting things
too man - y peo - ple at - tach - ing
string - - - - s I've got to spread my wing - - - - s
'cause I'm mov - - - in' on.
59
20
fade

Jazz waltz

Medium up swing (♩ = *ca.* 174)

I'm Movin' On
jazz waltz: Judy sings

61 I'm Movin' On
rhythm section alone: you sing!

We tried a more or less conventional jazz waltz pattern on **tracks 60-61**. Note Judy's fresh new start to the song. New styles of accompaniment will stimulate you to hear the song in new ways.

On the next page we can see from the transcription that Judy chose to come in on beat 2 of both ① and ② (page 31). Her entrance at ① has a more noticeable ascending slide of crescendo into "I've" whereas ② uses a brief upward slide into the word "I've."

Obviously you can't make any comping suggestions to the rhythm section in a pre-recorded track. However, as you sing along with **track 61**, listen closely to what the rhythm section is doing. If you like the way you can phrase over that accompaniment, you'll want to be able to explain the accompaniment to your rhythm section. After you've experimented with track 61 several times, just listen to the track alone. Let's analyze what the rhythm section is doing. Look at the bass line example above and listen to the intro in track 60. As you'll see, the piano and guitar figure bounces off the bass player's downbeats. The piano and guitar play together in the first measure, then the guitar continues this rhythmic pattern alone in each 2nd measure. This 2 measure pattern continues throughout the 8 measure intro. If the guitar figure kept going in every 2nd measure of the phrase under the melody, however, it would restrict your possibilities for phrasing the words in measures 2 and 6, etc. Our guitarist picked up on this immediately while comping behind Judy, and he changed his comping approach for the melody.

In ③ the piano continues its introduction pattern in the first bar of each 2 measure phrase while the guitar just adds long color chords:

In ④ the piano starts to change the pattern and ends up with the following figure variation for the first measure of the 2 measure phrase:

Also of interest: notice how the rhythm section expands their ideas for the last 6 measures once Judy sings her last word (measure 15 through 20) of ① and ②.

Note that the rhythm section comping is the same for ①, ③ and ⑤; ②, ④ and ⑥ are also identical.

Medium up swing (♩ = ca. 174) Jazz waltz
I'm Movin' On
Music by Kirk Nurock
Lyric by Judy Niemack
60
Intro
8
rhythm section
1
Gm11/D
Am11/D
I - - 've been col - lect - ing thing - s,
Gm11/D
Am11/D
too man - y peo - ple at - tach - ing string - - - - s
Cm11/F
B♭maj7/F
I've got to spread my wing - - s
Em11
Dm11
Em11
Dm11
2
'cause I'm mov - in' on.
2
Gm11/D
Am11/D
I've been col - lec - ting thing - - -
Gm11/D
(almost spoken)
Am11/D
- - s, too man - y peo - ple at - tach - ing string - - - s,
Cm11/F
B♭maj7/F
I've got to spread my wing - - s 'cause
Em11
Dm11
Em11
I - 'm - mov - - in' on.
61
Dm11
2
3
20
4
20
5
20
6
20
fade

Medium Latin

What would we get if we not only slowed the tempo down, but also changed the character drastically? How would this sound as a medium Latin? The results show, everyone liked it.

62 I'm Movin' On
straight trumpet melody (see the music on page 21)

With this approach, the melody could be played "straight" the way it was notated in the original lead sheet on page 21. Listen to the rhythm section and trumpet on **track 62**.

63 I'm Movin' On
medium Latin: Judy sings

Now listen to Judy interpret the medium Latin tempo (**track 63**, page 33). This new style gives her many new rhythmic ideas.

64 I'm Movin' On
rhythm section alone: you sing!

The slower tempo and even eighth notes of Latin percussion elements present a totally different framework. Some of Judy's rhythmic ideas became more complex, as in measures 3 ① and 15 ②. Simple quarter notes as expressed in the original melodic outline will also sound great (in ① see measures 2, 11, 14; in ② see measures 6, 10 and 11).

As Judy starts her second count-off measure, notice that the drummer immediately jumps in with a set-up that tells us the eighth note feel is going to change. It's now Latin, so the "feel" is going to be even eighths. Notice Judy's use of even eighths and precise downbeats, especially the measures starting with her "'cause" pick-up to measure 13 in ②.

Measure 14 of ②: The hyphen between the two "m's" is to help illustrate that she really only sings one "m." Here she uses the "m" rhythmically to show us both the downbeat ending of "I'm" and the 2nd beat start of "movin'."

This version at a slower tempo gives the vocalist more time to alter or emphasize certain notes or words. This slower tempo also offers different opportunities for vocal embellishments. Judy often elongates words to change the emphasis: "I've" in measure 1 of ① is longer than it's been in other examples. Notice how Judy varies the rhythms and accentuates each syllable in the first 4 measures of ②.

I'm Movin' On
Music by Kirk Nurock
Lyric by Judy Niemack
Medium Latin (♩ = ca. 130)
63
Intro
rhythm section
Gm11/D
Am11/D
I - 've been col - le - c - ting thing - - - s,
too ma - ny peo - ple at - tach - ing string - - - - s,
Cm11/F
B♭maj7/F
I've got to s - pread my wings 'cause
Em11
Dm11
I'm mov - in' on.
I've been col - lect - ting things
too ma - ny peo - ple at - tach - ing string - - -
- s, I - 've got to spread my wing - - - s 'cause
I - - 'm - mo - vin' on.
64
fade

Medium slow Latin

65 I'm Movin' On
medium slow Latin: Judy sings

66 I'm Movin' On
rhythm section alone: you sing!

How about an even slower Latin tempo, a real groove Latin feel? Notice how the drummer again sets up even eighths as he prepares for the first downbeat of the Intro.

Judy wanted to improvise vocally over the introduction to help her get into this new mood (**tracks 65-66**).

Notice the interesting syllables that Judy introduces in her vocal improvisation. Rhythmically, she gets right into the even eighth Latin groove. Listen to how she divides the last "y-a" to end her first phrase on the downbeat.

Measure 11 of (1) is complicated to look at, including very unconventional hyphenation. It's our way of pointing out how she continues the eighth note phrasing.

The song has a fresh new sound in a slow Latin groove. The rhythm section lays down a delicate and elastic background while the bass establishes a firm foundation and the drummer complements the texture with light rim shot patterns. The slower tempo means more space for dynamics and expression. Everyone listens and responds sensitively.

Sometimes songs sound great in entirely different moods than they were originally conceived. A "medium slow Latin" feeling is light years away from a "bright jazz waltz" feeling, but both work with this song. It was exciting for all of us to come up with new ways to experience ***I'm Movin' On***.

Medium slow Latin (♩ = ca. 108)
I'm Movin' On
Music by Kirk Nurock
Lyric by Judy Niemack
65
Intro
rhythm section
hoo vo deh ay ya deh deh yay ya y - a
bo do day ay ya da
I - 've been col - lect - ing
thing - s, too man - y peo - ple at - tach - ing string - - s,
I've got to s - pr - ead m - y wing - s 'cause I - 'm
mo - vin' on.
I - - 've been col - lec - ting thing - - s,
too man - y peo - ple at - ta - ching string - - s,
I got - ta s - pread my w - ings 'cause I - 'm
mo - vin' on.
66
fade

Smooth jazz

67 I'm Movin' On
smooth jazz: Judy sings

68 I'm Movin' On
rhythm section alone: you sing!

We asked for one last example to further widen our perspective. How about something with a smooth jazz flavor (**tracks 67-68**)?

Judy was stimulated to come up with fresh ways to explore the song, again improvising over the introduction. We asked Judy to write out syllable notation for her improvised intros (pages 35 and 37). No attempt has been made to notate the subtle horn-like articulations and nuances that she creates with her unique choice of syllables.

The drummer sets up a double-time feel with the cymbal pattern. In (3) when the guitar takes on more of a rhythmic comping role, the piano is freer to add solo fills around the melody.

To summarize: We all felt this was a rewarding experience, to explore different musical environments while spontaneously improvising new ways to think about the song. All of the suggestions we tried put smiles on everyone's face; all the musicians had fun responding to each other in a creative environment.

There are numerous ways to think about every song. Know the strengths of your rhythm section accompanists and incorporate those strengths in your own arrangement suggestions. If you have a certain style in mind, make sure you communicate that style clearly to your accompanist(s). Listen to their stylistic suggestions as well. Experiment. Try to be objective as you evaluate the results.

67
Medium up swing (♩ = ca. 164) Smooth jazz
I'm Movin' On
Music by Kirk Nurock
Lyric by Judy Niemack
Intro
rhythm section
soo va dool ya da do deh deh deh do do yo do vaw 'n deh deh 'n daw
deh deh 'n daw yoo deh deh bo doo ba yoo yoo deh doo do
so va yo ya yeh 'n deh do veh doo ya do da ya ah ya
I - 've been col - lec - ting thing - - - s, too man - y peo - ple at -
- ta - ching string - s I've got to spread my w - ing - s 'cause
I - 'm mo - vin' on.
I've been col - lec - tin' thing - s
a too man - y peo - ple a - ta - ching string - - s, well
I got to spread my wings 'cause I'm mo - - - vin'
on.
68
fade

Ballads

Ballads are challenging open phrasing songs. Every note has to mean something. You must convey the lyric, telling the story in your own way, and make it believable to your audience.

Giving a convincing ballad performance is a challenge to both instrumentalists and vocalists. Some instrumentalists feel it's very important to know the lyrics of the ballads they perform. Others don't investigate the lyrics, instead concentrating on interpreting the melody in his or her own personal way. Instrumentalists can stray further from the notated rhythm and melody than vocalists in most cases, because vocalists must make the lyrics meaningful with their embellishments and improvisations. Telling a convincing story should always be the ultimate goal for the singer.

Tadd Dameron, one of jazz's most influential composer/arrangers, wrote this next song. The opening section of the ballad ***Never Been In Love*** can be phrased in many different ways, depending on how you want to tell the story. Here is the basic melody, as it appears in ***Sing JAZZ!***

Sing through the lyric in this basic rhythm. In this song, your goal is to convince the audience that you've "never been in love" and let them know how you feel about it.

Giving more rhythmic length to a syllable or word will emphasize it. Listen to Gloria's "Nev-er" in measures 1 and 5 of ① (track 69). Now listen to "been" in measure 3.

Singing the words more rapidly can bring a different emphasis to the message. Listen to "with an-y-one" (measure 6 into 7 of ①, track 69), "Nev-er been in love" in measure 3 of ② (track 71) and measures 1 and 3 of ③ (track 73).

The following three music examples show different ways to phrase the melody. Listen to Gloria's interpretation in each, then try it her way yourself on the track that follows. Also create your own interpretations around the pianist's improvisations in tracks 70, 72 and 74.

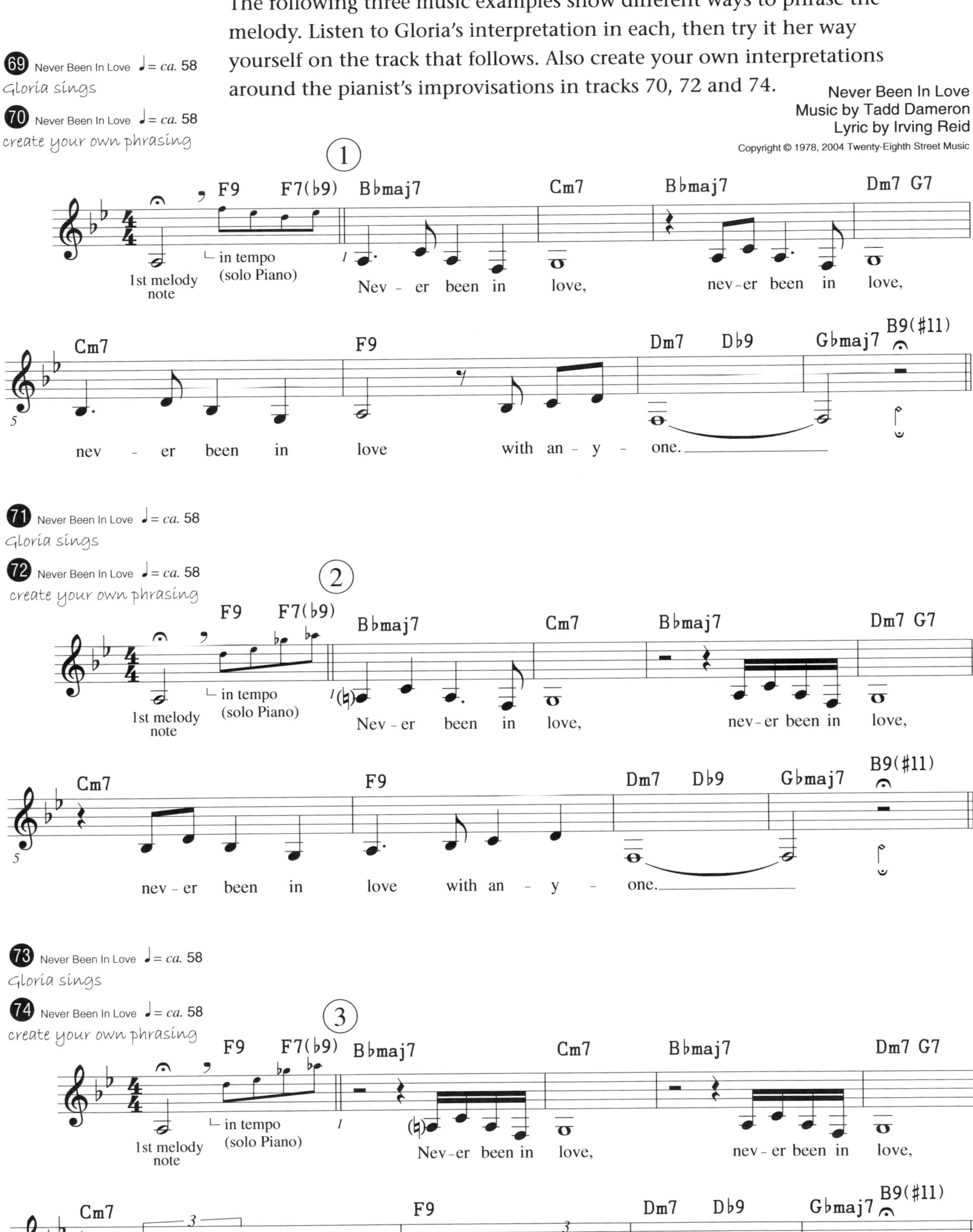

The musical examples below show variations of the first two measures of the song, illustrating some more musical ways to express "Nev-er" and to connect "never" to "been." Note how each new rhythmic environment creates a slightly different thought. However you phrase it, be convincing and believable in delivering your message.

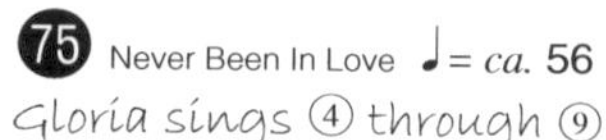
75 Never Been In Love ♩= ca. 56
Gloria sings ④ through ⑨

76 Never Been In Love ♩= ca. 56
your turn to sing ④ through ⑨
and create your own variations

Never Been In Love
Music by Tadd Dameron
Lyric by Irving Reid

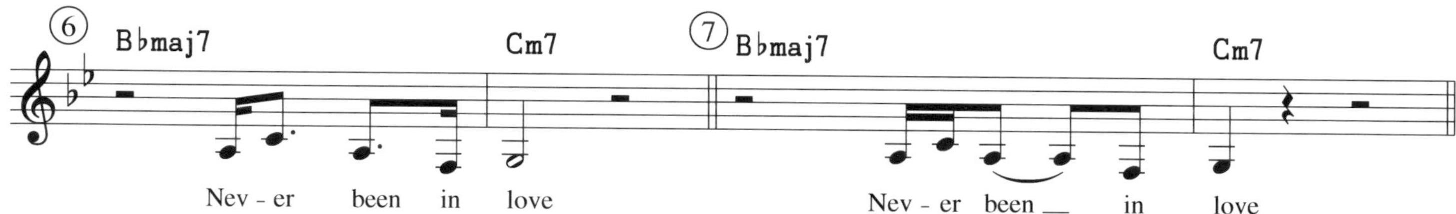

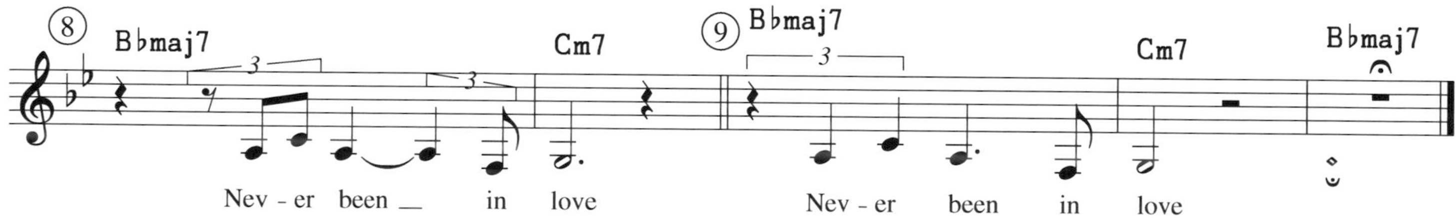

To summarize: Ballads are very popular with singers and audiences. Good ballad singing requires great control and sensitive phrasing. A great ballad performance can easily be the high point of your concert or set. Understand the story of the song, then work on ways to express the story in your own unique way. You and your accompanist(s) must listen carefully to each other and respond musically. The audience will appreciate the intensity and intimacy as you make music together.

Working On A Complete Arrangement

Now that you've convinced your audience of your plight, that you've "Never been in love," we'd like to give you something to pick up your spirits before the end of our musical journey. Let's lighten up and have some fun.

Hank Mobley was an important jazz tenor saxophonist and prolific composer who played and recorded with practically all of the jazz greats who were active during his playing career. Hank got so much of his music recorded because he had the knack of writing music that not only really fit with the various leaders he recorded with, but also music that communicates with the audience. It's hard to not start tapping your foot or snapping your fingers to Mobley's music. Guaranteed, his music will put a smile on your face. George V. Johnson put some fun lyrics to Hank's instrumental composition ***Comin' Back*** that George calls ***Your Day Is Comin'***, and you'll have a chance to sing it yourself.

Your Day Is Comin' is essentially a specific rhythm song with different accompaniment rhythmic feels behind different sections.

- The accompaniment for the introduction starts with a *rhythmic pedal* (pedals are repeating single bass note patterns).
- The melody at Ⓐ (page 44) has a *shuffle feel*, best thought of as an exaggerated triplet feel. More like ♪. ♬ than ³♩ ♪ in the drummer's cymbal pattern. A shuffle often has a 4-feel (the bass would "walk" 4 beats to the bar.) This time it has a *2-feel*, so the bass lays down a 2-to-the-bar feeling.
- The bridge, Ⓑ, is *4-feel*; the bass walks and the drummer swings "time," catching the indicated rhythmic figures.
- The *shuffle 2-feel* returns at Ⓒ .
- The **solo** section is all *4-feel*. There are two 32-measure solo choruses in this arrangement, [1] and [2] (pages 46-47).
- The repeat of the melody returns to the *shuffle 2-feel* at Ⓐ, then the *4-feel* bridge, then the *2-feel shuffle* at Ⓒ.
- The Coda goes back to the *rhythmic pedal* to end the song.

77 Your Day Is Comin'
trumpet plays the intro and the opening melody

78 Your Day Is Comin'
3 measures before the solo section [1] Solos

79 Your Day Is Comin'
pick-up to return of melody

80 Your Day Is Comin'
1 measure before the Coda sign (to Coda and ending)

The trumpet plays the entire arrangement (**track 77** segues through **track 80**, pages 44-47). Become familiar with the melody by singing along with the trumpet (**track 77**, music on pages 44 and 45) until you feel you have the melody pitches together. The introduction (and the ending) are especially challenging when you sing alone with the rhythm section track because no other instrument plays the melody with you, and there are no harmonies under you to help you hear your melody notes. We've provided the first two melody notes on the CD before tracks 77 and 82, so be sure to get them in your ear before you try to sing the intro. In performance with your own group, if there isn't an instrumental introduction to set up your first melody note, have someone in your group play your opening pitch (in this case the first two notes) before the downbeat.

Before exploring the **solo** section (pages 46 and 47, **track 78**), let's review some basic terminology regarding musical form and chord progressions.

Analyzing the form

Your Day Is Comin' is a song with an introduction, melody, solo section, a repeat of the melody, and a Coda (ending). The music is on pages 44-47.

Intro: a specific written introduction, 16 measures long.

melody: The melody starts with a one note pick-up to measure 1 and continues through measure 30.

The melody fits into what is called a 32 measure, AABA song format. In this song each section is 8 measures long.

The first A (measures 1 through 8);
the second A (measures 9 - 16), a repeat of the A melody with a new lyric and new melodic material in the 2nd ending;
the **bridge** (B, measures 17-24);
and the last A, at rehearsal letter Ⓒ (measures 25-32).

The melody is over in measure 30 of the A section. The last two measures of the last A section (measures 31-32) are a drum solo which sets up the solo section.

Solos The two solo choruses use the same chord progression as the AABA melody. The chord progressions of all the A sections are essentially the same. The chord progressions of all the bridges (B) are the same. The written melodic lines in the two solo choruses will be discussed on page 43.

return to the melody: The pick-up to the melody is the last beat of measure 96. The instruction *D.S.*𝄋 *al* 𝄌 means return to the sign 𝄋 (at Ⓐ) for what we call the "out melody" then skip to the Coda when you see the Coda sign 𝄌 at the end of measure 30.

Coda: The 𝄌 **Coda** shows the 2 measure drum solo which is still part of the last A section. The Coda officially begins with "Your eyes," which starts with the same melody that was used in the introduction. The song ends with a hold (*fermata* 𝄐) on the word "bye" in the last measure of the Coda.

About the solo section

For most jazz musicians, improvised solos are what jazz is all about. A solo section is vital to a jazz arrangement. Jazz soloing is all about interaction—the soloist and the rhythm section tell a spontaneously created story together. The soloist is creating a new melody based on the chord progression of the song, which the rhythm section is playing. "Taking a solo," for those of you new to jazz, means scatting or vocalizing your own melodic material over the "changes," a common reference to the solo section chord progression. In the arrangement of ***Your Day Is Comin'*** in this book, a soloist would "take 2 choruses" after the melody is stated. Each solo chorus utilizes the chord progression of the song (AABA). In track 83 you can hear the rhythm section alone backing the 2 solo choruses without a soloist.

Knowing your "changes" (chord progression). To take a meaningful solo, you must always be aware of the chord progression as you're creating your new melody.

78 Your Day Is Comin'
trumpet plays background figures during the solo section

If you're not comfortable as a jazz soloist yet, look at the melodic lines we have created in solo choruses 1 and 2 (pages 46 and 47) and listen to the trumpet play them (**track 78**, which starts 3 measures before the solo section). These melodic lines are simple, and every A section is different. The numbers written under the staff analyze the notes in relation to the chord symbols: the 3 under the first note in measure 33 means that the note, D, is the 3rd of a B♭7 chord, and so on. "Root" refers to the bottom note of the chord. Thirds (3) and sevenths (7) are very important in defining harmonic relationships.

Backgrounds behind soloists have often been used in jazz. They are supporting melodic and rhythmic statements played behind a soloist. A background should stimulate the soloist to come up with new ideas. Riff figures (short repeating figures) are commonly used as background material. A background could be just a recurring riff figure.

Look at the melodic lines in solo choruses 1 and 2 (pages 46-47). We have purposely filled them with lots of riff figures. Examine measures 41-42, 49, 57-58, 65-66, 73-74, starting with the 3rd beat of 80-81, 89-90.

Bb

Your Day Is Comin'

Music by Hank Mobley
Lyric by George V. Johnson

Instrumentally known as "Comin' Back"

* circled notes are bass notes

Your Day Is Comin' - page 2 **(B♭)**

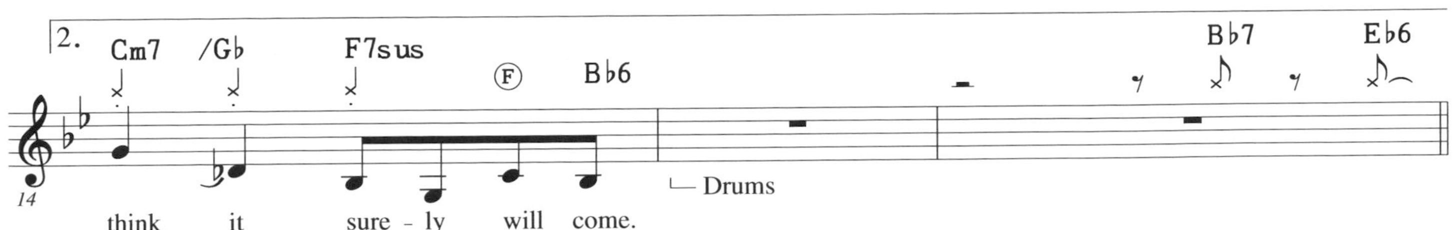

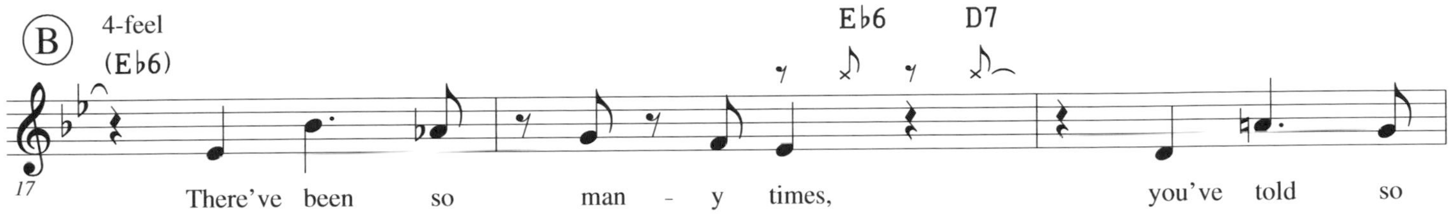

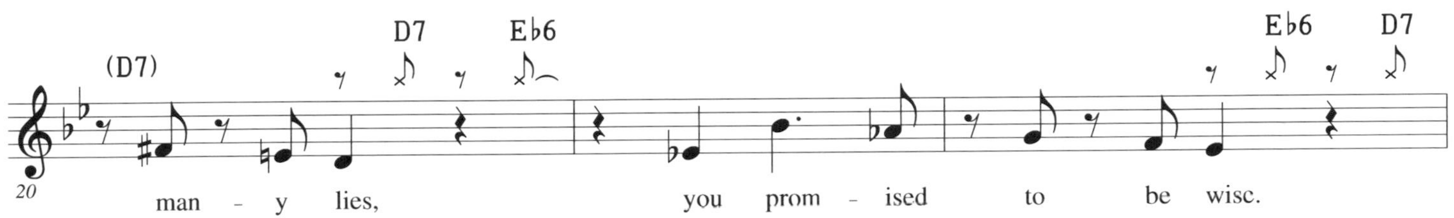

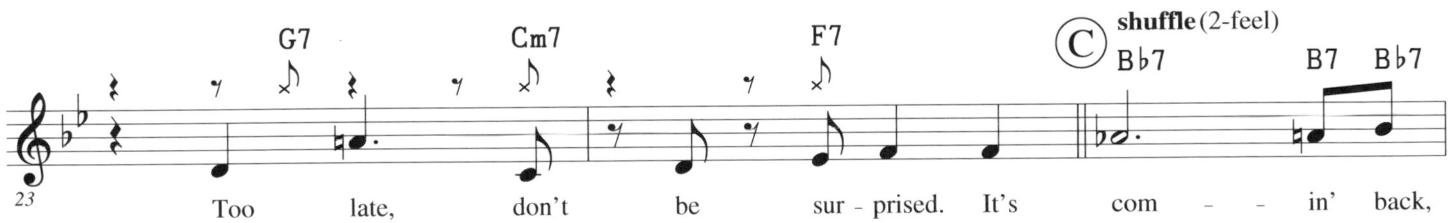

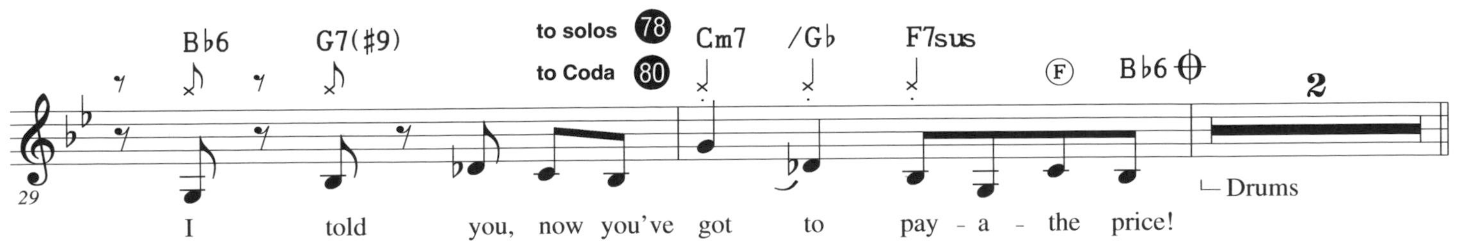

* A passing tone, not a chord tone. In this case it's the 4th note of the B♭ scale.

Your Day Is Comin' - page 4 (B♭)

* chromatic upper neighbor followed by chromatic lower neighbor to the 3rd

Creating backgrounds

Let's start by discussing backgrounds behind the A sections of a soloist. Most of the individual A sections of [1] and [2] ([A1], [A2], [A3] and [A4]) shown on pages 46-47 could be used as independent 8-measure A section backgrounds for an entire solo chorus. Sing any one of these A sections with the rhythm section for every A section in **track 83**, leaving the bridges open. Try the other A sections with track 83 in the same manner. If you continue the basic 2-measure riffs started in [A5] (measures 73-74, page 47) and [A6] (measures 89-90) throughout the full 8 measures, they will also work as individual backgrounds for all the A sections of a chorus.

83 Your Day Is Comin'
2 chorus solo, rhythm section only

Backgrounds often work best if they are not behind every section of the soloist's chorus. A common 1 chorus background consists of a repeating A section background, with the bridge left open for just the soloist. If your soloist doesn't mind a background behind two choruses of his or her solo, try the following 2 chorus background formula. Sing your first A section background. Repeat it again for the next A section. Leave the bridge open for the soloist (no background). Then sing the original A section background for the last A section of the first chorus. On the soloist's second chorus, leave the A sections open for the soloist and sing a background for the bridge. Try either [B1] or [B2] as a bridge background (pages 46-47).

81 Your Day Is Comin'
trumpet plays simplified background during the solo section

Backgrounds can be fun to create. In [3] and [4] below we've drawn material from [1] and [2], reorganized and sometimes simplified the lines to create two other full chorus background treatments. The trumpet plays these backgrounds on **track 81**. If you are ready to take your own solo, try to solo over [3] and [4] on track 81.

Your Day Is Comin'
Music by Hank Mobley
Lyric by George V. Johnson

B3
Eb7
D7
Eb7
D7
G7
Cm7
F7
Bb7
Eb7
Bb6
G7
Cm7
F7
Bb6
(Cm7
F7)
4
Bb7
Eb7
Bb6
G7
Cm7
F7
Bb6
1.
(Cm7
F7)
2.
Bb7
B4
Eb7
D7
Eb7
D7
G7
Cm7
F7
Bb7
Eb7
D.S. al
Bb6
G7
Cm7
F7
Bb6
(Cm7
F7)
(page 44)
It's

Some soloists like to "stretch out" and take several solo choruses. A background is often used as a signal to a soloist that his or her last chorus is starting (or the second-to-last chorus in a 2 chorus background set-up). For a 2 chorus background, you could also try the reverse of the background formula on page 48: play a background for the bridge only of the soloist's next-to-last chorus, then play a background for each of the three A sections in the last chorus, leaving the bridge open.

Try to re-arrange the melodic material from [1] and [2] into different A section backgrounds. Create your own background riffs and section backgrounds and try them with the other melody instrumentalists in your ensemble.

Backgrounds should be in every vocalist's survival kit. Solo improvisation choruses are fundamental to jazz. Someone has to "solo." If you perform this song with your own group, someone will have to "take a solo" before you come back in with the melody and lyric for the out chorus. If you're not a soloist, and you have several soloists in your group who are eager to take solos, it may be a long time before you get to sing again. Jazz soloing is all about interaction, and a way you can interact with the soloist is to sing a background behind the solo. You could sing the background by yourself, but if you have several instrumentalists in your group, a unison background where you blend with another instrument could sound great.

82 Your Day Is Comin'
intro and opening melody

83 Your Day Is Comin'
downbeat of solo chorus [1]

84 Your Day Is Comin'
out melody at (A)

85 Your Day Is Comin'
Coda

You can sing the whole arrangement with just the rhythm section (**track 82** through **track 85**). The music is continuous (these tracks segue). For practice purposes, track 82 is the introduction and opening melody and tracks 83 through 85 identify the different sections. Track 83 starts right at [1] of the solo section, so you can easily repeat this section at will to practice soloing or to try your background riffs. Track 84 starts at (A), the downbeat of the out melody. Track 85 starts at the Coda sign.

What have we learned about jazz phrasing?

Before you try to perform a song, first think of the song in terms of the composer's tempo/style indication on the lead sheet. After you've examined the composer's suggested tempo/style, do you hear it differently? As a ballad? A medium tempo swing? In some type of Latin context? As an uptempo swing? How do you hear it?

Next, consider if there are sections that require specific rhythm phrasing to maintain the integrity of the song. Try to identify these sections, respect the melody and rhythms, and learn how to make them work for you and your ensemble.

How do you approach the eighth notes in a song? Tempo, style and, of course, experience will help you decide (swing eighths, even eighths, etc.) Listen to other artists, both vocalists and instrumentalists, and try to analyze their phrasing.

If there are open phrasing sections, be creative and experiment with several ways to phrase them. Use the approach that is most comfortable for you and yet expresses the emotions you want the lyric to convey.

Some songs are quite flexible and can be performed in many different ways. There is nothing wrong with trying a new approach to a song to see if it works. Songs identified as open phrasing songs, like most ballads, offer the widest variety of approaches.

Learn how to communicate with your ensemble so they can provide the best support for your performance.

Through looking at music notation, analyzing it and, *most importantly*, listening to recorded examples, you can gain valuable insight into the world of jazz phrasing. Sing-along examples afford you the opportunity to learn and experiment at your own speed.

Remember, the way you phrase a song brings it to life!

Vocal and Instrumental Discography

The vocal version title is listed first, with its recordings. If the vocal version hasn't been recorded, the instrumental title and its recordings follow immediately. If there is no indication of an instrumental recording, the title has not been recorded as an instrumental. The format is leader / title of album or CD (company and number [alternate release company and number]). Although not all of these recordings are in print, we have attempted to list currently-available release numbers.

Rob Bargad
12 Another World

Pamela Baskin-Watson
58 Love We Had Yesterday, The

Walter Bolden
26 Do It Again (with R. Rachel Mackin)

Ruby Braff
106 We're All Through

Clifford Brown
18 Beloved (with Meredith d'Ambrosio)
108 When We're Alone (with Michael Stillman)

Donald Brown
40 I Love It When You Dance That Way (with Donald & Dorothy Brown)

Oscar Brown_Jr.
36 Honeydo

Ray Bryant
62 Meant To Be! (with Fleurine)
72 One Fine Day (with L. Aziza Miller)

Jon Burr
82 Sea Breeze

Sara Cassey
104 Warm Blue Stream (with Dotty Wayne)

Paul Chambers
20 Chillin' (with R. Rachel Mackin)

Michael Cochrane
100 Two Reflect As One (with Cheryl Pyle)

Al Cohn
102 Underdog, The (with Dave Frishberg)

Tadd Dameron
68 Never Been In Love (with Irving Reid)
94 There's No More Blue Time (with Georgie Fame)

Walter Davis_Jr.
16 Being Such As You, A

Kenny Dorham
30 Fair Weather
80 Rhyme Of Spring (with Meredith d'Ambrosio)

George Duvivier
11 Alone With Just My Dreams

Curtis Fuller
59 One Dream Gone (with Fleurine)
91 Sweet And True (with Catherine Whitney)

Mathew Gee
70 Oh! Gee!

Rodgers Grant
34 Gift Of Love, The
76 One Heart's Dream (with Catherine Whitney) lyricist

Wardell Gray
95 Twisted (with Annie Ross)

Al Grey
57 Love Is Forever (with Meredith d'Ambrosio)

CONTAINS COMPLETE VERSIONS OF THE SONGS EXPLORED IN THE Jazz Phrasing Workshop

The ***Sing JAZZ!*** songbook contains music composed by some of the world's finest jazz composers and performers. Many of the selections were originally instrumental compositions; however, in this volume they appear as songs with lyrics. With its unique emphasis on selections drawn from the astonishingly rich world of instrumental jazz, ***Sing JAZZ!*** opens up a completely new range of repertoire for the vocalist. The table of contents shows both the lyricized title and the original "instrumentally known as" title. A separate index by instrumental title is included. ***Sing JAZZ!*** thus provides an opportunity to explore classic jazz material in a new and exciting way. A helpful hints section has detailed information on notation, style and form, as well as insights into performance techniques. The lyrics are shown under the music and are also presented separately, in a "lyrics alone" section. Brief biographies of the composers provide a historical context. Several indexes (by composer, lyricist, original instrumental title, and tempo/style) allow easy access to the material.

LYRICS TO THE MUSIC OF RENOWNED JAZZ ARTISTS ROB BARGAD ◆ PAMELA BASKIN-WATSON WALTER BOLDEN ◆ RUBY BRAFF ◆ CLIFFORD BROWN ◆ DONALD BROWN OSCAR BROWN, JR. ◆ RAY BRYANT ◆ JON BURR ◆ SARA CASSEY ◆ PAUL CHAMBERS MICHAEL COCHRANE ◆ AL COHN ◆ MEREDITH d'AMBROSIO ◆ TADD DAMERON WALTER DAVIS, JR. ◆ KENNY DORHAM ◆ GEORGE DUVIVIER ◆ CURTIS FULLER MATTHEW GEE ◆ RODGERS GRANT ◆ WARDELL GRAY ◆ AL GREY ◆ JOHNNY GRIFFIN GIGI GRYCE ◆ FLETCHER HENDERSON ◆ EDDIE HIGGINS ◆ LONNIE HILLYER BERTHA HOPE ◆ ELMO HOPE ◆ SHEILA JORDAN ◆ JONNY KING ◆ HAROLD LAND MELBA LISTON ◆ CURTIS LUNDY ◆ RONNIE MATHEWS ◆ TOM McINTOSH SERGIO MIHANOVICH ◆ HANK MOBLEY ◆ GRACHAN MONCUR III ◆ J.R. MONTEROSE RALPH MOORE ◆ KIRK NUROCK ◆ JOHN ODDO ◆ FRITZ PAUER ◆ CECIL PAYNE BOBBY PORCELLI ◆ JULIAN PRIESTER ◆ FREDDIE REDD ◆ RENEE ROSNES CHARLIE ROUSE ◆ MILTON SEALEY ◆ NORMAN SIMMONS ◆ LUCKY THOMPSON BOBBY TIMMONS ◆ TOMMY TURRENTINE ◆ MAL WALDRON ◆ CEDAR WALTON ROBERT WATSON ◆ CHUCK WAYNE ◆ SCOTT WHITFIELD ◆ JAMES WILLIAMS

SUNG BY CLAUDIA ACUÑA ◆ ERNESTINE ANDERSON ◆ LENY ANDRADE ◆ CHET BAKER JERI BROWN ◆ OSCAR BROWN, JR. ◆ BETTY CARTER ◆ GLORIA COOPER MEREDITH d'AMBROSIO ◆ DENA DeROSE ◆ KURT ELLING ◆ GEORGIE FAME ◆ FLEURINE DAVE FRISHBERG ◆ BILL HENDERSON ◆ EDDIE JEFFERSON ◆ SHEILA JORDAN ◆ IRENE KRAL LAMBERT, HENDRICKS & ROSS ◆ JEANNE LEE ◆ ABBEY LINCOLN ◆ GLORIA LYNNE KEVIN MAHOGANY ◆ TINA MAY ◆ JANE MONHEIT ◆ MARK MURPHY ◆ JUDY NIEMACK ANNIE ROSS ◆ VANESSA RUBIN ◆ JIMMY SCOTT ◆ DARYL SHERMAN ◆ BEN SIDRAN CAROL SLOANE ◆ MARY STALLINGS ◆ TIERNEY SUTTON ◆ TUCK & PATTI ◆ SARAH VAUGHAN DINAH WASHINGTON ◆ AND MANY, MANY MORE!

Also in *Sing JAZZ!*
- **Tempo/style index**
- **Vocal and Instrumental discography**
- **Biographies**
- **Glossary**
- **Indexes by composer and lyricist**
- **Index by original instrumental title**

Each leadsheet includes
- **Suggested tempos and styles**
- **Chord symbols**
- **Accompaniment rhythm indications**
- **Rehearsal letters**
- **Measure numbers**
- **Recording credits**

Available from
your local music dealer
Distributed by Hal Leonard Corp.

price $14.95
Product number 00740213

About The Composers . . .

WALTER BOLDEN, drummer with many jazz greats for over 50 years until his death in 2002, worked with Stan Getz, Horace Silver, Gigi Gryce, Gerry Mulligan, Sonny Rollins, Ray Bryant, George Shearing, Art Farmer, Annie Ross and others. In the late 1970s, he contributed many originals to Taylor's Wailers, a group led by his close friend and legendary jazz drummer, Art Taylor.

CLIFFORD BROWN was an amazing trumpet player and composer. He was in the limelight for just five years, yet his mark on jazz is indelible. Early performances at jam sessions with Dizzy Gillespie, Charlie Parker and Fats Navarro (his major influences), led to work with Lionel Hampton and Tadd Dameron through 1953. Brown was then heard briefly with Art Blakey before teaming with Max Roach to form their heralded quintet. Fortunately, Clifford was able to make quite a few recordings before his untimely death. His compositions have become jazz classics.

TADD DAMERON was one of jazz' most influential composers and arrangers. Dameron had a wonderful melodic and harmonic imagination which he brought to compositions and arrangements for both small and big bands. Writing first for Harlan Leonard, Jimmie Lunceford and Billy Eckstine, he then composed and arranged for Dizzy Gillespie's big band in the late 40s. He led and recorded with his own superb sextet that often featured trumpet great Fats Navarro. Dameron wrote compelling songs and arrangements for John Coltrane, Sonny Stitt, trumpeter Blue Mitchell and many others.

CURTIS FULLER is probably the most influential of modern trombonists, after J.J. Johnson. Born in Detroit, he moved to New York in 1957, where he played and/or recorded with Miles Davis, Gil Evans, John Coltrane (including the famed "Blue Train" session), Bud Powell, the Jazztet, Quincy Jones, Sonny Clark and many more. Later, Fuller performed in Art Blakey's Jazz Messengers (1961-65, 77-78) and was a sideman with Count Basie, Benny Golson and others. He has recorded widely as a leader and currently leads his own sextet.

BERTHA HOPE was born and raised in Los Angeles. She began studying classical piano with her parents at the age of 3. Hearing Bud Powell on recordings and in person convinced her to try to play jazz piano. Her pursuit included 6 months of piano lessons with Richie Powell, Bud Powell's brother. In 1958 she met her husband, pianist/composer Elmo Hope, when he came to L.A. as part of Sonny Rollins' group. Since Elmo's death in 1967, Bertha has worked to keep his legacy alive while pursing her own pianist/composer playing and recording career.

HANK MOBLEY, tenor saxophonist and composer, left an important legacy of recordings and compositions. Musicians loved him. Horace Silver called him his hippest tenor soloist. Early appearances and recordings with Max Roach and Dizzy Gillespie led to his teaming in 1954 with Kenny Dorham, Silver, bassist Doug Watkins and Art Blakey to form the Jazz Messengers. Many recordings as a sideman, including Miles Davis, and as a leader on the Blue Note, Savoy and Prestige labels.

KIRK NUROCK is a talented composer and pianist whose interests range from contemporary music and jazz to "cross-species" explorations. Son of a jazz pianist, Nurock studied at the Juilliard School and at the Eastman Arranging Laboratory. He has played with Dizzy Gillespie, Sonny Stitt, Phil Woods, and Lee Konitz, and has written songs for singers Theo Bleckmann and Sheila Jordan. He is also active as an educator.

CHARLIE ROUSE, a distinctive tenor saxophonist, played in the 40s and 50s with Dizzy Gillespie, Billy Eckstine, Tadd Dameron, Fats Navarro, Duke Ellington, Clifford Brown and many others. He formed The Jazz Modes with French horn player Julius Watkins. Rouse is probably best known for his lengthy tenure (1959-70) with Thelonious Monk.

TOMMY TURRENTINE, a marvelous musician and composer, was the elder trumpet-playing brother of tenor saxophonist Stanley Turrentine. After initially working with Benny Carter, saxophonist Earl Bostic and Count Basie, Turrentine performed and/or recorded with Max Roach, Horace Parlan, Sonny Clark, Jackie McLean, Lou Donaldson, Dexter Gordon and Big John Patton.

. . . Lyricists . . .

MEREDITH d'AMBROSIO Singer/pianist/composer, d'Ambrosio is an artist whose original songs and lyrics to those by others always have a deep ring of truth. Her classical and jazz studies in the late 40s and early 50s made her a resourceful pianist. A leader since the mid-50s, she often accompanies herself. Meredith has released numerous fine albums on the Sunnyside label.

GEORGE V. JOHNSON, a fine singer as well as lyricist, worked with James Moody's band in the 1980s. Recently, George was one of the featured artists in a week-long festival of Hank Mobley's music, where George sang his lyrics to over 20 Hank Mobley compositions.

R. RACHEL MACKIN's songs and lyrics have been performed on television and in jazz clubs and concert halls. As a pianist, Rachel played in New York City hotel lounges and private clubs, as well as on cruise ships for the Cunard Line. She studied jazz piano with Sanford Gold and voice with Barry Harris in his jazz workshops.

L. AZIZA MILLER, a former music director and pianist for Natalie Cole, has appeared as a vocalist with Ahmad Jamal. Her lyrics to Milton Sealey's compositions have been recorded by singer Jeri Brown. English vocalist Tina May has recorded "One Fine Day," Miller's lyric to Ray Bryant's jazz classic "Cubano Chant."

JUDY NIEMACK's first major performance was a week at the Village Vanguard with Warne Marsh in 1978, which was also the year of her first recording. Since then she has performed in most of the major clubs in New York City, as well as many international venues. She now lives in New York City and Berlin, Germany, where she heads the Pop/ Jazz Vocal Department at the Hanns Eisler Music Conservatory.

IRVING REID A gifted lyricist who worked extensively in musical theater, Reid collaborated with Tadd Dameron and many others. His works range from popular music (some recorded by Perry Como) to jazz to sacred.

BEN SIDRAN discovered jazz in the 1950s. A pianist, producer, singer and composer, he has recorded and produced recordings for such noted artists as Van Morrison, Diana Ross, Mose Allison, and Jon Hendricks. He has authored books on the subject of jazz and is recognized as the host of National Public Radio's landmark jazz series "Jazz Alive," which received a Peabody Award.

CATHERINE WHITNEY is a Chicago-based vocalist/composer/lyricist and multimedia producer who comes from a long line of published poets. Catherine's lyrics have been recorded by singers Jeri Brown, Gloria Cooper and others.

. . . Musicians . . .

VINCE CHERICO Drummer Cherico has been performing in a variety of musical settings since arriving in New York City. He is currently a member of The Ray Barretto Sextet and has performed with Ray Bryant, Kenny Burrell, The Caribbean Jazz Project, Paquito D'Rivera, Brian Lynch, James Moody, The New York Voices, Dave Samuels, Mongo Santamaria, and Ray Vega.

CECILIA COLEMAN Pianist, composer and bandleader Coleman is a native of Long Beach, California and also a resident of New York City. Coleman has led her own group since 1990. She has performed at the Monterey Jazz Festival, the Telluride Jazz Festival and the New Mexico Jazz Workshop. She is currently the jazz piano instructor at CSU Long Beach, California. Coleman has four albums as a leader.

AKIL DASAN has played music since childhood. Currently teaching and performing in the New York/New Jersey area, he studied composition at Columbia University. His primary instruments are the guitar and vocals (including vocal percussion), which he blends into a unique style influenced by classical, jazz, soul, hip-hop, funk and other contemporary genres.

ANGELA DeNIRO DeNiro is a native New Yorker. In addition to jazz singing, she has done extensive studio work, with various jingles to her credit. She is currently performing in New York jazz clubs with both the Ron Aprea Big Band and her quintet. In January, 2001, DeNiro performed on the nationally televised competition "Jazz Discovery" on BET-TV, and won first prize.

TIM GIVENS Originally from California, bassist Givens moved to New York City in 1988 and has played with Lou Donaldson, Ray Bryant, Curtis Fuller, Billy Mitchell, Frank Vignola, Richie Cole, Jesse Davis and many others.

JEANFRANÇOIS PRINS A jazz guitarist originally from Belgium, Prins started playing music at the age of 17. He has performed as a leader and/or sideman with Toots Thielemans, Lee Konitz, Judy Niemack, Kenny Wheeler, Bud Shank, Fred Hersch and many others. Prins has recorded five CDs as a leader. He is currently teaching guitar at the Hanns Eisler Music Conservatory in Berlin, Germany.

. . . and Authors

DR. GLORIA COOPER An impressive jazz pianist and vocalist who is also an esteemed academician, Dr. Cooper has had a lengthy and fruitful career as both a performer and an educator. She has performed with such musicians as Eddie Harris, Red Holloway, David "Fathead" Newman, Jimmy Witherspoon, Meredith d'Ambrosio, Gloria Lynne and others. She earned her doctorate in music and education from Columbia University's Teachers College in 1992. Cooper's CD, "Day By Day," was released in 2001 on GAC Music and includes Eddie Henderson on trumpet, Yoron Israel on drums, and Ron McClure on bass. She is currently Assistant Professor of Music at Long Island University in Brooklyn, New York. Dr. Cooper is the editor of ***Sing JAZZ!***

DON SICKLER Widely known in a variety of jazz roles: performer (trumpet/flugelhorn), arranger, transcriber, producer, conductor, publisher, educator. Sickler started to gain recognition as a performer, arranger and transcriber with Philly Joe Jones in the late 70s. His playing and arranging has varied from the big bands of Art Blakey and Clifford Jordan to many smaller groups, including a Monk All-Star Tentet; Birdology; Monk On Monk, T.S. Monk Sextet, Billy Higgins Sextet and Harold Land/Billy Higgins quintet. Currently writing for and playing in the Curtis Fuller Sextet and Ben Riley Septet. Sickler has five leader CDs. Over 250 recorded arrangements, including arrangements for singers Betty Carter, Meredith d'Ambrosio, Nneena Freelon, Shirley Horn, Abbey Lincoln, Kevin Mahogany, Maria Muldaur, Diane Reeves. Producer of many CDs (including 5 Grammy winners), also recent CDs for vocalists Carol Sloane and Mark Murphy. As conductor, projects with Diana Krall, Dee Dee Bridgewater, Jane Monheit and many others. Sickler teaches at Columbia University and remains active as a publisher.